RULERS OF INDIA

RULERS OF INDIA

The Marquess of Hastings, K. G.

BY

MAJOR ROSS-OF BLADENSBURG, C.B.

GYAN

Published by

Gyan Publishing House
5, Ansari Road
Daryaganj, New Delhi-110002
Phone: 011-47034999, 9811692060
E-mail: books@gyanbooks.com

Distribution Network
gyanbooks.com
India, USA, Canada, UK, Australia

ISBN: 978-93-6208-505-4 (HB)
First Published, 1893

2nd Impression 2024

Printed at: Gyan Press, Delhi.

RULERS OF INDIA
Author: MAJOR ROSS-OF-BLADENSBURG

Rulers of India

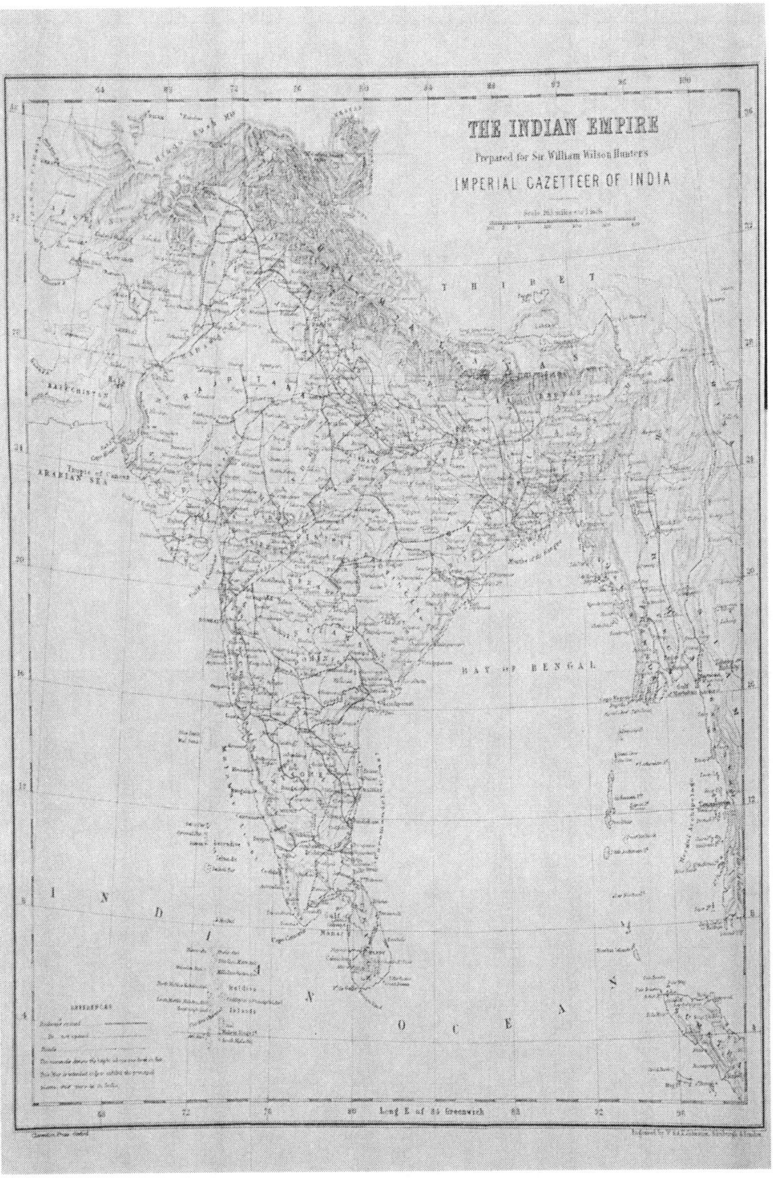
THE INDIAN EMPIRE
Prepared for Sir William Wilson Hunters
IMPERIAL GAZETTEER OF INDIA
THIBET
BAY OF BENGAL
ARABIAN SEA
INDIAN OCEAN
Long E. of Greenwich

Hastings

RULERS OF INDIA

The Marquess of Hastings, K.G.

By MAJOR ROSS-OF-BLADENSBURG, C.B.
COLDSTREAM GUARDS

Oxford
AT THE CLARENDON PRESS: 1893

PREFACE

In compiling the following sketch of the Indian Administration of the Marquess of Hastings, I have devoted a few pages to the history of that celebrated soldier and statesman, both before and after the period of his rule in the East. In this part of my work, I have been much assisted by Lord Donington, who most kindly placed at my disposal some notes on the life of his distinguished relative.

The rest of the volume is partly drawn from Mr. Prinsep's *History of the Political and Military Transactions in India during the administration of the Marquess of Hastings*, 1813–1823, 2 vols., London, 1825. Many of the military details of the Pindárí and the third and last Maráthá war have been taken from Colonel V. Blacker's *Memoir of the operations of the British Army in India during the Maráthá war of* 1817, 1818, *and* 1819, London, 1821. The numerous other authors consulted are referred to in the foot-notes of the following pages.

J. R. of B.

Rosstrevor House, Co. Down,
September, 1892.

CONTENTS

NOTE

The orthography of proper names follows the system adopted by the Indian Government for the *Imperial Gazetteer of India.* That system, while adhering to the popular spelling of very well-known places, such as Punjab, Poona, Deccan, &c., employs in all other cases the vowels with the following uniform sounds:—

a, as in wom*a*n: *á*, as in f*a*ther: *i*, as in k*i*n: *í*, as in intr*i*gue: *o*, as in cold: *u*, as in b*u*ll: *ú*, as in r*u*ral.

LORD HASTINGS

CHAPTER I

Family History. War of American Independence, 1754—1781

Francis Rawdon-Hastings, afterwards Marquess of Hastings and the Governor-General of India, whose administration there forms the subject of the present memoir, was born on the 9th of December, 1754. He was the eldest son of John Lord Rawdon by his third wife, Lady Elizabeth Hastings (eldest daughter of Theophilus, ninth Earl of Huntingdon), who, upon the death of her brother, the tenth Earl, in 1789, succeeded to many of the honours and to all the estates of the Hastings family; these she transmitted to her son Francis, who assumed his mother's surname in addition to his own, and thus united in his own person the representation and the traditions of two illustrious families.

The Rawdons derive their ancestry from Paulyn de Rawdon, who is said to have commanded a body of archers at the Battle of Hastings, and was rewarded by considerable grants of land in Yorkshire, part of which called Rawdon gave the surname which the family assumed. The successors of this Norman maintained their position in the county, and to the present day his representative, Lord Loudoun, has portions of the Conqueror's original grant in his possession[1].

Nineteenth in direct descent from Paulyn, George Rawdon settled in Ireland, where he took a prominent part in the rebellion of 1641 as an officer of merit, and afterwards in the affairs of that country; he was created a Baronet of England in 1665, being denominated of Moira, Co. Down, where his Irish estates lay. His son, Sir Arthur, was distinguished in the troubles of 1688–89, siding with William; and his great-grandson, Sir John Rawdon, was elevated to the peerage of Ireland in 1750, as Baron Rawdon of Rawdon, Co. Down, and eleven

[1] The lands appertaining to the Manor of Rawdon are held by a very curious old rhyming Title-deed which is supposed by some to date from the Conqueror, and which runs as follows:—

I William Kyng, the thurd yere of my reign
Give to the Pawlyn Roydon, Hope and Hopetowne
With all the bounds both up and downe;
From Heven to Yerthe, from Yerthe to Hel
For the and thyn, ther to dwel,
As truly as this Kyng right is myn;
For a crosse bow and an arrow
When I sal come to hunt on Yarrow.
And in token that this thing is sooth,
I bit the whyt wax with my tooth,
Before Meg, Mawd, and Margery,
And my thurd sonne, Henry.

years later was created Earl of Moira in the same peerage. He married three times, without male issue by his first and second alliances, but by the third marriage he had, together with other children, a son, Francis, whose career we are about to describe.

The house of Hastings owes its origin to Robert, Portgrave of Hastings (whence the family name was taken), and dispensator or steward of William the Conqueror. The elder branch of the Portgrave's descendants rose to considerable eminence in the earlier part of English History; one of them, John de Hastings, became Seneschal of Aquitaine, and was in 1290 an aspirant to the throne of Scotland in right of his grandmother Ada, daughter of David Earl of Huntingdon, and niece of Malcolm IV and William the Lion, kings of Scotland. The grandson of this Baron, was Laurence, who was created Earl Palatine of Pembroke in 1339, as representative of his great-uncle, Aylmer de Valence, son of William, half-brother of Henry III. That dignity expired in 1389, upon the death of Laurence's grandson, and the elder branch of the Hastings family became extinct; but a younger branch survived, and soon became distinguished in the person of Sir William de Hastings, who was born in 1430.

This Knight was a staunch adherent of the House of York, and upon the accession of Edward IV to the throne was rewarded for his services in the civil war by appointments to many positions of trust and emolument, by large grants of the forfeited estates of the Lancastrians, and by a peerage (Barony of Hastings of Ashby de la Zouche), 1461. Hastings, moreover, acquired additional gifts of land through his wife; and by his ability, bravery, and fidelity to his sovereign, he became one of the foremost and most influential persons in the kingdom. As Master of the Mint he introduced a new gold coinage; as a trusted ambassador he took part in missions to France and Burgundy (sometimes for the development of British trade in Flanders); and as a military commander he was present at the decisive battles of Barnet and Tewkesbury. He was instrumental in bringing Clarence to the king's side just before the battle of Barnet, where Warwick was killed and his schemes annihilated, and he was present at the interview between the two brothers which led to so important a result. His end is well known, and has been pourtrayed by Shakespeare in 'King Richard III,' who took the story of his dramatic death from Sir Thomas More's account as described by Cardinal Morton, an eye-witness to the scene. Hastings was jealous of the queen and of her brother Rivers, but nothing could shake his loyalty to his master's son, Edward V; the Regent Gloucester, unable to bribe him, caused his murder in the Tower, 1483.

Hastings' son, Edward, increased the family honours by his marriage with Mary, sole heir of Thomas, Baron Hungerford; and his grandson George, a favourite of Henry VIII, was created Earl of Huntingdon, 1529. The latter was succeeded by Francis, who married Katherine, eldest daughter of Henry Pole, Lord Montacute, and niece of Cardinal Pole, and hence granddaughter and representative of Margaret, Countess of Salisbury, daughter and heir of George, Duke of Clarence, brother of Edward IV. Francis attached himself to the fortunes of Warwick, afterwards Duke of Northumberland, and thereby obtained advantages in lands and appointments. To consolidate this alliance he married his heir Henry to his leader's daughter, on the same day that Lady Jane Grey married Lord Guilford Dudley. Huntingdon was fortunate enough, however, not to be involved in Northumberland's fall, and to escape after a short imprisonment; he was doubtless protected by his fortunate marriage, by which he gained the interest of Cardinal Pole, nor is it improbable that he was shielded from harm by the influence of his brother who was a strong partisan of Queen Mary; he was able to conceal his religious opinions in those troublous times, but in his heart he appears to have inclined to Protestantism.

His daughter Mary received the doubtful compliment of an offer of marriage from Ivan IV (the Terrible) of Muscovy, 1583, which, strange to say, seems to have been favourably entertained by Elizabeth, though it was known that the Tsar had a wife living whom he proposed to repudiate; it is needless to say that the offer was rejected by the lady[1].

[1] Those who are interested in this curious portion of Anglo-Russian History should consult Karamsin, *Histoire de l'Empire de Russie, traduite par M. St. Thomas*, Paris, 1820, vol. ix. chap. 7.

Henry, son of Francis, succeeded his father as third Earl; he claimed succession to the throne after Elizabeth, in right of his mother; and in the troubles then raging between religious opinions and the claims of heredity, his pretensions were supported by a considerable section of the Protestant leaders during the severe illness of Elizabeth in 1562. By religion he was a zealous puritan, a strong sympathiser with the Huguenots, and he 'much wasted his estate by a lavish support of those hot-headed preachers.' He had something to do with the persecution of Mary Queen of Scots, but he had the good sense to perceive that honour, if not policy, must prevent a rival to the throne from taking too open a part against her. He died without issue in 1595, and was succeeded by his brother, whose great-grandson Ferdinando, sixth Earl, flourished in the reign of Charles I, and was brother to Henry, the celebrated Lord Loughborough, an ardent supporter of the king. Ferdinando's son adhered to the cause of James II, and protested against the Act of Settlement, 1701; he was eventually succeeded by his son Theophilus as ninth Earl, who was the father of Lady Elizabeth, third wife of Lord Moira (John, Lord Rawdon), and mother of Francis, the future Ruler of India[1].

Such in brief is an account of the families from which Rawdon sprang, and such some of the traditions which he represented and inherited. But there

[1] Dictionary of National Biography, vol. xxv. London, 1891, pp. 115-135; *Hastings*. Burke's *Peerage*. Lodge's *Peerage of Ireland*, 1789.

were other influences around his youth which helped to shape his mind. Among his ancestors there had been persons of religious zeal and of learning; his mother is described as having had a strong natural understanding, cultivated by a very refined taste; her own mother, Selina, daughter of Lord Ferrers, was a person of remarkable talent and character; she became the patroness of the Methodist reformers (Wesley, Whitfield, &c.) and devoted herself entirely to good works, founding the sect of methodists known as 'Lady Huntingdon's Connection,'—a religious association at that time much despised by the upper classes of society.

Francis Rawdon, who in 1761 became known by the courtesy title of Lord Rawdon, was educated at Harrow, when Dr. Sumner was Head Master, and where he was one of the pupils of Dr. Joseph Drury. He evinced early a strong desire to devote himself to a military career, and was gazetted Ensign in the 15th Foot in 1771, at the age of seventeen; shortly afterwards he matriculated at University College, Oxford, but took no degree there. Having made the usual continental tour, which in those days was considered to give the finishing touch to the education of a 'young gentleman of quality,' he was promoted to a lieutenancy in the 5th Foot in 1773, and embarked immediately for America to take part in the War of Independence.

He spent nearly eight years in America, and there he gained his first great experiences of life. When he landed (about the beginning of 1774) the colonists were seething in excitement; the cargoes of tea had just been destroyed at Boston, and the crisis was about to reach its climax,—soon to be solved by war. In the troubles that followed he distinguished himself, and displayed qualities of no mean order; he had to undertake responsible duties, and these he discharged with ability, firmness, and courage; in America he laid the foundation of his subsequent career. The school in which he received this early training, was one of adversity and depression, well nigh of despair. The struggle was a fratricidal one; the British commanders were men of inferior capacity; the support they received from home was half-hearted; they were opposed to leaders of energy and of genuine enthusiasm; they were confronted by a hostile population which refused to be conciliated and which was not to be trusted.

The British army, unaccustomed to reverses, was harassed and humiliated; raw levies were gaining on seasoned troops; battle after battle was won by the British forces, and yet no advantage followed; skirmishes were lost, and immediately the Royalists had to evacuate a province. No progress was made, and finally the Colonies separated themselves for ever from the British Crown.

Rawdon took part in the Battle of Bunker's Hill in June, 1775, where he first saw active service, and there he displayed such conspicuous gallantry as to attract special notice from General Burgoyne, who in a letter written to England said, 'Lord Rawdon has this day stamped his fame for life.' A month later he was promoted Captain in the 63rd Foot, and soon afterwards was appointed aide-de-camp to Sir Henry Clinton. The following year he was present at the taking of Brooklyn, at the action of the White Plains, and was with the invading column under Lord Cornwallis which temporarily subjugated New Jersey and reached Trenton.

In the year 1777 he was again with Cornwallis when Philadelphia was occupied, and there he raised a Regiment of Irish Volunteers, drawn from the same sources from which the American levies were mainly recruited. He commanded this regiment till he left the country in 1781, and under his leadership it greatly distinguished itself, especially at the Battles of Camden and Hobkirk's Hill, where it lost heavily. Rawdon had, however, great difficulties with his men at first, owing to the numerous desertions that occurred among them; but he soon put an end to this trouble, by the following expedient. A man was caught in the act of going over to the enemy; instead of trying him by court-martial, Rawdon brought him on parade before the whole regiment, and delivered him over to his comrades, in the most impressive way, to be judged, and punished or acquitted. The officers were all ordered to withdraw, and in a short time the offender was convicted and immediately hanged on the next tree. Desertion thenceforward was almost unknown among the men of the Irish

Volunteers[1]. In June, 1778, Philadelphia was evacuated and a retreat effected to New York; Cornwallis commanded the rear guard, and Rawdon, who was still with him, took part in the action of Monmouth (28th June).

By this time he had been promoted Lieut.-Colonel, 15th June, and shortly afterwards he was appointed Adjutant-General to the British Forces in America. The same year (1778) Georgia had been cleared of the enemy; but it was not until the end of 1779 that the departure of the French Fleet enabled Sir H. Clinton, the Commander-in-Chief at that time, to proceed with the subjugation of the southern provinces. Clinton sailed from New York, and reaching Charleston, to which he proposed to lay siege, ordered Rawdon to join him there with a brigade of some 3,000 men. The trenches were opened before the town in April, 1780, and the place taken in May, after which three columns were sent to Camden, Ninety-Six, and Augusta, to occupy the Colony. Clinton then returned to New York, leaving Cornwallis with 4,000 regulars to hold the conquered districts and to reduce North Carolina to the King's authority. Rawdon remained in the south, and was ordered to Camden in command of the advanced troops near the frontier between the two Carolinas.

His task was a trying one, for the Americans under General Gates collected a strong force with secrecy, and were bearing down upon him; meanwhile

[1] The Annual Biography and Obituary, for the year 1828, xii. 144.

Sumpter, a determined Colonial leader, at the head of some partisans, attacked a post at Hanging Rock, on the 6th August, and nearly captured it. This news brought Cornwallis to Camden, where Rawdon was concentrating his forces and constructing defensive works, and on the 16th, Gates was engaged and was completely defeated, losing all his artillery and most of his baggage. Two days later Sumpter's force was also cut to pieces [1].

No victory could be more complete, and Cornwallis now determined to advance into North Carolina; but his force was weak, sickness prevailed, and transport was deficient. He met with little resistance, and was pushing on towards Salisbury, when he heard of the total destruction, 9th October, at King's Mountain, of a body of Loyalist Militia, nearly 1,000 strong, under Major Ferguson, who had pursued an American partisan force which was forming near Ninety-Six. The disaster dispirited the royalists and obliged the British to retire; the retreat was not effected without loss, provisions failed, the roads were almost impassable, and the hostile militia hung upon the march; Cornwallis was suffering from fever, and so the command devolved upon Rawdon. On the 29th October, Winnsborough was reached and the army was reformed.

Clinton having heard of the success at Camden,

[1] Bancroft's *Hist. of the United States*, London, 1874, x. 309, &c. The Cornwallis Correspondence, 3 vols., London, 1859, i. 55, &c., and Appendix, Nos. II. and III.

sent General Leslie with 2,000 men to create a diversion on the Chesapeake, but eventually this reinforcement was landed at Charleston on the 13th December, and a fresh advance was made into North Carolina in January, 1781. The campaign began inauspiciously, for a detachment covering the left flank suffered a severe defeat at Cowpens, by which some 600 men were lost, 17th January; the march was nevertheless continued, and after an action on the Catawba, Hillsborough was occupied, 20th February. Cornwallis now hoped to be able to rally the royalists of North Carolina, but he failed, as they were either disheartened or non-existent, and owing to the energy of the American general, Greene, his supplies were cut off and his levies dispersed. He was now obliged to fall back upon the Deep River, but not for long, for, advancing again towards Guilford, he met Greene at the head of 5,000 men, and defeated him, 15th March. This victory was entirely useless, and four days later Cornwallis, perceiving that his force was inadequate to maintain its position, and that the Royal cause was without hope in the colony, took the desperate step of retreating down Cape Fear river, and reached Wilmington on the 7th April, with little more than 1,000 men. On the 25th he finally abandoned the southern provinces by marching northwards along the coast to Virginia, to effect a junction with another British force which had been sent to the Chesapeake to co-operate with him from that direction.

Meanwhile Rawdon was left in command in South

Carolina with five regiments of regulars and ten provincial corps. Communications with the main army were fairly secure until the middle of March, when all trace of it was lost and Rawdon had to act for himself. Cornwallis did not disguise from himself that he left the troops in the south in great danger, and exposed to attack from Greene who was free to operate against them. He had good cause for extreme anxiety, for Rawdon's position was most critical; the British forces were weak, the country to be held was large, and the detachments necessarily far apart, a hostile column was in front, irregular detachments were threatening the flanks, and the population was rising in the rear. A few points only of the interesting operations which followed can be noted here, but sufficient, it is hoped, to show the temper and the quality of the man (who was in the future to govern the Indian Empire), when pitted against the general considered by the Americans to be second only to Washington himself.

Rawdon's first care was to concentrate, and he resolved to do so at Camden; but before he could accomplish this operation, Greene appeared in the neighbourhood with 1,800 men. Fearing lest he should soon be reinforced, and seizing a favourable opportunity, the British commander advanced with only 800 men, and surprised him at Hobkirk's Hill, where he was strongly posted (25th April). The British troops took a circuitous route through thick woods, and were obliged to move on a narrow front; the enemy, having barely time to form, met the attack by grape, and under cover of their artillery, attempted to charge; but the assaulting columns were immediately deployed, and having very soon dispersed the Americans, the latter were defeated with loss. Brilliant as the success was, it brought Rawdon only a small measure of relief, for the province was swarming with the enemy's partisans and post after post was capitulating; he profited by his victory, however, in so far that he completed his concentration (7th May), and then having made a dash at Greene, he evacuated Camden and crossed the Santee river. Arrived there, he heard the worst accounts of the state of the province; the revolt was universal, and Charleston itself was not free from danger, but being of opinion that offence is good defence, he recrossed the Santee to disperse the enemy who were now gathering thick about him. He could get no information from the inhabitants, and his difficulties were increasing, so much so that believing Greene had got round his rear, he retraced his steps and took up a position at Monks Corner, where he covered Charleston.

The important post at Ninety-Six was by this time completely exposed to the enemy, and was invested by Greene, 22nd May. Rawdon had previously sent many messengers by various routes to the commandant ordering him to evacuate it, but none of these reached their destination. To add to his troubles the British Army, notwithstanding its exhausted condition, had been further weakened by the absence of a regiment which he sent to Savannah, where the royalists were in great difficulties. It was therefore most fortunate when three Irish regiments landed at Charleston on the 3rd June. Rawdon, now able to act, advanced promptly with this unexpected reinforcement to Ninety-Six, where he raised the siege, and then pursued the enemy for forty miles beyond that station, while they, not venturing even to meet him, retreated with the utmost precipitation. Ninety-Six was evacuated like Camden, and as the arrangements were being carried out by the commandant, Rawdon marched with 800 men, and a few horsemen, to harass Greene still further, and ordered a detachment from Charleston to join him for this purpose on the 3rd July.

The order miscarried, and Greene intercepting a messenger, knew it had miscarried; he accordingly hoped to surround the British commander, but the latter moved so rapidly that he missed his chance, and only captured a few dragoons. When too late, and when the English did eventually receive some reinforcements, he came up with them (10th July), but having reconnoitred their position, he found it too strong and retreated again in haste. Shortly afterwards the detachment from Ninety-Six reached the British lines; and thus the bulk of the army in South Carolina which, in April, was scattered through a hostile province, in isolated bodies and opposed to a formidable enemy, was withdrawn from its perilous position, and was, in July, safely reunited and concentrated near Charleston, by the prudence and energy of its young commander[1].

The war now languished; the Americans occupied the high hills of the Santee; the British held the line of the Santee, the Congaree, and the Edisto; both sides were exhausted, and the weather was oppressively hot. Rawdon, whose health had broken down, was obliged to return to Europe. The ship he sailed in was captured by a French cruiser, and he was taken to Brest; but being soon exchanged, he reached England in safety. In November, 1782, he was promoted Colonel, and appointed aide-de-camp to the King.

Although he naturally acquired great credit from his gallant conduct in America, yet he was accused of having dealt harshly and cruelly with the enemy. This charge was baseless, but nevertheless it gave him considerable pain. In February, 1782, a motion was defeated in the House of Lords, by a very large majority, by which it was sought to condemn the execution of a certain American, Isaac Haynes, who was taken in arms after having given his parole; Rawdon, who was in command at the time, and who really sought to save the man, was so incensed at this reflection upon his character, that he demanded and obtained a public apology from the mover. Those who have read Bancroft's account of the war, will perceive that it contains assertions of

[1] Annual Register, 1781 (*Hist. of Europe*), chap. v. Bancroft's *Hist of the United States*, x. 483, &c.

British cruelty and of American forbearance. Impartial readers will probably form a more moderate opinion, and conclude that in all civil wars—where feeling runs high, and where the population is drawn into the struggle—there is likely to be some harshness on both sides. In fact, if the Americans had to complain, so also had the English military authorities bitterly to protest against the barbarities practised by their opponents.

But the most important accusation comes from Washington, who, in October, 1780, wrote to Clinton impeaching the acts of both Cornwallis and Rawdon; as Washington was not opposed to those commanders at the time, it is to be inferred that he spoke not of his own knowledge, but reproduced what others (not so fair-minded perhaps as himself) had reported to him. Both the officers concerned vehemently repudiated the aspersions cast upon them, and Rawdon remarks sarcastically, 'the rebels have by the rigour of their administration reaped too many advantages over our forbearance to wish that we should affect more energy[1].' Even Bancroft does not deny that treachery was practised against the British, and quotes a case with apparent satisfaction, where a militia commander waited till his men were supplied with arms and ammunition, and then conducted them over to the enemy[2]. This was no solitary instance; on the contrary, constant and persistent efforts were

[1] Cornwallis Correspondence, i. 60, 72, 501.

[2] Bancroft's *Hist. of the United States*, x. 313.

made to undermine the allegiance of the royalist levies. The English, therefore, were merely carrying out the ordinary customs of war, adopted by all belligerents for their own protection, and they had necessarily to punish spies and those who deserted or caused others to desert. Had the commanders not taken effective means to repress this class of perfidy, which occurs too often in all civil wars, they would have failed in their duty; to accuse them of want of humanity is the mere trick of an interested partisan.

CHAPTER II

FURTHER MILITARY SERVICES; POLITICAL LIFE; APPOINTED GOVERNOR-GENERAL OF INDIA

1781—1813

WHEN a man has greatly distinguished himself in his youth, and has proved himself in later years to be a statesman of capacity, an administrator of merit, and a ruler of energy, it is not often that his middle life should be nearly a blank. Yet this is what happened in Rawdon's case, for from 1781 to 1812, though he performed acts worthy of notice, he made no persevering effort to cultivate his natural endowments, and never rose above mediocrity. Nor were opportunities wanting, for it was precisely in those years that talent had a full field for labour; and as, by his family connections and by his personal character, he was in a position to obtain and profit by high employment in the public service, so is the break in his career which now took place all the more remarkable.

On reaching England, he found that in his absence in America he had been returned member for Randalstown, Co. Antrim, to the Irish House of Commons, and early in 1783 he was raised to the peerage of Great Britain under the title of Baron Rawdon of Rawdon, Co. York; but beyond speaking against Fox's India Bill in December, he appears during four years to have taken little part in politics. Meantime he became warmly attached to the Prince of Wales and to his cause; he gradually estranged himself from Pitt, whose party he had at first supported, and in 1787 he openly joined the opposition. He was certainly ambitious, and dreamt of power, but he also sought and stipulated for independence, and he endeavoured to make a position for himself, with a party of his own, by coming prominently forward to advocate the interests of the Prince on the Regency question. The recovery of the King, early in 1789, frustrated the hopes he entertained, and he does not appear again in political life until 1797. He still, however, took an interest in some public questions, and, in 1793, attempted unsuccessfully to alter the harsh laws then prevailing against insolvent debtors.

On account of his intimacy with the Prince of Wales and his brothers, and it is stated by some, at the personal request of the King, he acted as second to the Duke of York in the duel which took place between the latter and Colonel Lennox (afterwards Duke of Richmond), in May, 1789. He maintained afterwards that having delayed the signal, he rendered Lennox's aim unsteady, and thus saved the life of the Duke who had determined not to fire at his opponent[1].

By the death of his father, June 1793, Rawdon succeeded as second Earl of Moira in the peerage of Ireland. In the following October he was promoted Major-General, and shortly afterwards he undertook an expedition to La Vendée, to support the attempt there being made to overturn the revolution in France. This expedition proved a failure and the troops did not even land; one of the bravest of the insurgent chiefs, La Rochejaquelein, had just been killed, and disunion reigned among the remainder, the people at that time distrusting them so far as to imagine that their leaders would desert in the British ships.

The next year, the army in Flanders under the Duke of York was in difficulties; the allies, among whom there was little concerted action or cordiality, were being driven back by the ardour of the revolutionary armies of France. On the 18th May the Duke was defeated, and although he avenged this reverse four days later, yet he became involved in the general disasters of the campaign. Ypres fell on the 17th June, and the British were obliged to retreat upon Oudenarde and on the 3rd July upon Antwerp. On the 26th June the battle of Fleurus made the position of the allies desperate. Lord Moira was about this time encamped near Southampton with

[1] An interesting and detailed account of this celebrated duel is to be found in Colonel Mackinnon's *Hist. of the Origin and Services of the Coldstream Guards*, ii. 30.

10,000 men, preparing for a secret expedition to France. The disasters in Flanders, however, caused his destination to be changed. He sailed to Ostend, and landing towards the end of June, he determined to push on at once to the assistance of the Duke. Ostend had to be evacuated, and the French entered it the same day, 1st July, the garrison being transferred by sea to Flushing; but, before that date, Moira started into the interior, and after a most difficult march, through a country already in the possession of a victorious enemy, he got into communication with the Austrian general, Clerfayt, who, astonished at his success, greeted him with the following not undeserved compliment: '*Vous, milord, avez su faire l'impossible.*' He reached Alost, on the 6th July, but there he was immediately attacked by the French. His troops were much exhausted by their rapid and hazardous march, and the enemy forced an entrance into the town, but he succeeded in driving them out, and on the 8th he joined the Duke of York. They then held the Brussels-Antwerp canal, when, on the 12th, their position was assaulted, and they were driven to Malines; Moira, upon this, made a gallant counter-attack, and forced the enemy to retire, but three days later he was again obliged to withdraw into Malines, which, being untenable, was evacuated, and the troops were brought to Antwerp, which was still held to cover the movements of the Dutch.

This very interesting military episode, in which

Moira displayed his old prudence and spirit, led to a very unfortunate occurrence. One method taken to pass unchallenged along the front of the French army was to deceive the latter by making them think that a much stronger force was advancing to the support of the Duke of York than was actually the case. Moira gave orders to collect rations for 25,000 men during his march, and Pichegru, who commanded the enemy at Bruges, believing that this was the real strength of the forces opposed to him, did not interfere with their movements, when he might have prevented their advance. The *ruse* succeeded; but the British Government afterwards declined to pay the bill, and referred the contractor to the private purse of the British general, whence to recover the debt due for rations which had been drawn for 15,000 men who did not exist. Moira refused to pay, and nothing was done further in the matter till after his death, when his widow, having rendered herself liable for her husband's debts, by an undertaking which she executed in ignorance, was sued for the amount. Parliament was petitioned to discharge the money due, but in vain; and the result was that some thousands of pounds were exacted from Lady Hastings, to liquidate a charge which had been incurred for the benefit of the public service, and which had enabled the Duke of York to receive a substantial reinforcement when the British army under his command was in imminent danger.

The march from Ostend was the last active service

in which Moira was engaged until he went to India; for he appears shortly after the events just recorded to have left the seat of war. His subsequent military career at home is unimportant, and may be thus summed up: he was promoted Lieutenant-General in 1798, and General in 1803; he was appointed Commander of the Forces in Scotland about the same time, Colonel of the 27th Foot in 1804, and Constable of the Tower in 1806.

In 1797 Moira announced, in a letter to Colonel McMahon, that a large number of Members of Parliament who supported the Government had proposed that he should become Prime Minister to the exclusion of both Pitt and Fox, and he intimated that he was quite ready to form an administration if the King wished it, but that he declined to co-operate with the greater part of Pitt's colleagues, especially the Duke of Portland, and would only admit a few of Fox's friends; his Chancellor of the Exchequer was to be Sir J. Pulteney. This news, according to his critics, 'threw the whole town into paroxysms of laughter,' and drew the following remarks from his old friend and late commander, Cornwallis: 'It is surely impossible that Lord Moira's letter can be genuine; if it is, excess of vanity and self-importance must have extinguished every spark of understanding, and I am sure there was a time when he had sense [1].'

[1] Cornwallis Correspondence, ii. 329. Readers of the Poetry of the Anti-Jacobin will remember the 'Ode to Lord M—ra' written upon this occasion, of which the following is the last stanza:—

But although Moira did not excel as a parliamentary chief, and had possibly no capacity for the business, yet he took considerable interest in certain matters of supreme national importance, and formed strong opinions upon them which he urged with characteristic vigour and self-reliance. The state of Ireland at the end of the last century was a source of endless embarrassment to English statesmanship, and the difficulties of the situation, far from diminishing, became intensified day by day. Government, under the able administration of Pitt, had a distinct policy, but Moira was in independent opposition and felt that this was the moment for him to intervene. He had been trained in the depressing school of the American revolution, and, while as a soldier he did his duty, he could not but observe and meditate over the fatal consequences which followed the ungenerous and weak conduct of those ministers who contributed so much to bring about the disaster.

The state of Ireland seemed to him to be analogous to that of the late colonies which he knew so well, and having a seat in the Irish House of Lords as well as at Westminster, he frequently called attention to the affairs of that country. He urged that grievances

Old P-lt-n-y too your influence feels,
And asks from you th' Exchequer seals,
  To tax and save the nation:
T-ke trembles, lest your potent charms
Should lure C—s F—x from *his* fond arms,
  To YOUR Administration.

Poetry of the Anti-Jacobin, p. 55; Ed. Lond. 1799.

should be redressed, and resented the recall of Lord Fitzwilliam in 1794; he spoke of the poverty and the hardships endured by the Irish, and of the cruelties practised upon them by the military; he even went so far as to declare his opinion that unless grievances were put an end to, and the number of malcontents thereby reduced, Ireland would not remain connected with England for five years longer. He was a consistent advocate of Catholic emancipation, and frequently urged that important reform. He opposed the Union on the ground that it was not acceptable to the people, and voted against it in the Irish House, but, on its passing, he gave it his adhesion in the House of Lords at Westminster.

Conciliation is a wise policy, and the redress of grievances and of injustice the only true and proper solution in the case of general discontent; and Moira did well in denouncing the bigotry which prevailed against the Catholics, and in trying to improve the condition of the people; but he went too far, and was censured for it, when he was understood to justify, and therefore to encourage, the Irish Jacobin movement that broke out into a savage rebellion in May 1798[1].

[1] Moira's views received a rude, if not an amusing, illustration, when only a short time after making one of his most violent speeches against the Government, the rebels selected his demesne near Ballynahinch as their battlefield against the King's authority. The wits of the day thereupon composed 'A New Song' called 'Ballynahinch,' in which the following lines occur:—

The objects of Pitt were identical with his own, for both endeavoured to remove injustice and the causes of legitimate complaint; but Pitt had also to assure himself that he did not disturb the fundamental principles of law and order, without which no society can stand and all concessions must be useless. That Moira would have adopted a similar course, despite his speeches, is shown by the fact that although he denounced British rule in India as 'founded in injustice and originally established by force,' and opposed Lord Wellesley's policy there, he in no way guided his conduct by this opinion when the reins of government were placed in his own hands, and, on the contrary, shaped his action on the model afforded to him by the great Governor-General whom he had criticised.

When Fox and Grenville came into office, in 1806, Moira was admitted to the Privy Council, and was appointed Master of the Ordnance; but the following year he resigned office, when the Duke of Portland came into power—the same statesman whom he specially excluded from his projected ministry of 1797, but with whom on the Regency question in 1788 he had, in his own words, 'slidden into a kind of alliance.'

'Determin'd their landlord's fine words to make good,
They hid Pikes in his haggard, cut staves in his wood;
And attack'd the King's troops—the assertion to clinch,
That no town is so *Loyal* as Ballynahinch.

O! had we but trusted the *Rebels'* professions,
Met their cannon with smiles, and their pikes with concessions;
Tho' they still took an *ell*, when we gave them an *inch*,
They would all have been *Loyal*—like Ballynahinch.'

Poetry of the Anti-Jacobin, p. 214.

Towards the end of 1810 the king had another attack of his old malady, and an arrangement had to be made for the discharge of the Royal functions. It so happened that the party in power then was of the same complexion as that which had been in office twenty-two years before, when the question was first debated, and thus the same arguments were reproduced with the significant exception that the point maintained by Fox (that the Prince of Wales as Heir-Apparent succeeded by right to the Regency) was in this instance abandoned. As a result, however, the proposals of Pitt in 1788 were substantially carried, and the arrangement adopted remained effective. Moira, true to his affection for the Prince, took a prominent part in these proceedings, and supported him to the utmost of his power. Nor did his desire to be of service to the Regent end here, for he also took an active part on his behalf in the investigation of the conduct of the Princess; on account of which he was obliged to defend himself early in 1813 against the allegation that he had secretly attempted to obtain evidence against that unfortunate lady; these charges he strongly repudiated, and whatever might have been his anxiety to serve a Prince whose friendship and confidence he had enjoyed for many years, it is certain he was not the man to stoop to a low office such as had been suggested by his enemies.

His last performance in the political arena at home was perhaps the most important. An account of the interesting negotiations which took place with regard to a reconstruction of the cabinet in 1812 is impossible in a work of the present kind, but a brief outline of what occurred may be summed up as follows. Early that year Mr. Perceval's government was weakened by the resignation of Lord Wellesley, who thought the time had come for a settlement of Catholic claims, then hotly resisted by the ministers in power. An effort was now made to enlarge the administration, with a view to the consideration of these claims, and the Regent resenting the illiberality of the ministry and desiring to strengthen his hands by the assistance of 'some of those persons with whom the early habits of his public life were formed,' endeavoured to make it succeed; but it failed, and things went on as usual until May, when the Prime Minister was assassinated in the House of Commons. The leadership then devolved upon Lord Liverpool, who tried to obtain the support of Lord Wellesley and Mr. Canning to prop up his government, then considered in a tottering condition: this also failed. It soon became evident that the ministry could not command a majority in the House, and thereupon the Regent addressed himself to Lord Wellesley, who undertook to attempt to reconcile the chief members of both parties, on the basis of a conciliatory adjustment of Catholic claims and a vigorous prosecution of the Peninsular war. In a short time, however, he had to give up the task, and Lord Moira—who had helped him in his mission and who was to have had a seat in the proposed cabinet—was then sent for and empowered to conduct these delicate negotiations. Just at first it seemed as if he would succeed, for Lords Grey and Grenville, the principal persons concerned, agreed to his propositions; but a divergence of opinion soon became manifest on the question of the Household appointments, and as neither side would give way, the arrangements fell through. On the 8th of June Lord Liverpool announced that he had been appointed Prime Minister, and the crisis ended.

There were many who blamed Lords Moira, Grey, and Grenville for this collapse of Whig aspirations; the two latter, for allowing the regulation of the Household to stand in the way of all their political wishes; while of the former it was said, that to him alone was owing the continuance of a ministry whose removal he once said (not six months before) 'ought to be rapturously hailed by the whole country,' as by that event only could the Catholics get a prospect of obtaining a redress of their grievances [1].

But though the results of the negotiations just recorded caused disappointment to many who hoped to derive benefit therefrom, the confidence which the Prince Regent reposed in Lord Moira was not weakened, nor the friendship he entertained for him disturbed. He had conducted his difficult mission with zeal and ability coupled with singleness of purpose and firmness of will. Failure was not imputed to him, nor was he held accountable for the result of his

[1] *Annual Register*, 1812: (*General History*), pp. 45, 79, 129, &c.; (*State Papers*), pp. 329, 346, &c.

undertaking; on the contrary, the transaction raised his credit, for the Prince approved of his services and the ministers appreciated his character.

Shortly after these events he was installed Knight of the Garter, and on the resignation of Lord Minto was appointed Governor-General and Commander-in-Chief in India. He was eminently qualified for this high position; his energy and military ability, his strength of character and liberality of mind, his high personal integrity and scrupulous sense of honour, all rendered him peculiarly fitted to wield the great powers which were to be intrusted to his charge and to grapple with the questions that awaited his solution.

He sailed from Portsmouth on the 14th of April, 1813, and landed at Calcutta on the 4th of October, when he at once assumed his new functions. He remained in India till the 1st of January, 1823, and thus his rule there lasted a little more than nine years.

It will be convenient to conclude this chapter by a short account of the remainder of the personal history of the man who forms the central figure of the transactions described in the following pages; thenceforward his individuality becomes merged in the events which he controlled, and hence it will be useful to dismiss the person in favour of the work he achieved.

Lord Moira married, in 1804, Flora, Countess of Loudoun in her own right (only child of James, fifth Earl of Loudoun in the peerage of Scotland), by whom he had six children. His mother died in 1808, and upon that event he succeeded to the ancient baronies of Hastings, Hungerford, &c., which were vested in the Hastings family[1]. In February, 1817, he was created, on account of his public services in India, Marquess of Hastings, Earl of Rawdon, and Viscount Loudoun, in the peerage of the United Kingdom, and in 1818 he was made a G. C. H. and G. C. B. Several votes of thanks were passed in his favour in both Houses of Parliament, and the same was passed in the general Court of the East India Company in February 1819, when a grant of £60,000 was voted for the purchase of an estate for his wife and issue. After his death a further sum of £20,000 was also voted for the benefit of his son, who was then under age. When offered a Marquessate, he endeavoured to get the title of 'Marquess of Clarence,' and he based his request upon his descent from George Duke of Clarence, brother of Edward IV. But this application was not entertained, and the title conferred upon him was derived from the town in Sussex where his ancestor had been Portgrave in the reign of William the Conqueror. It appears moreover he had been led to believe that he would have been created a Duke at the coronation of George IV, but this expectation was not realised.

Lord Moira is described as a tall athletic man, dark

[1] The Earldom of Huntingdon descended in the male line only, and became suspended for some years after the death of Lady Moira's brother, until claimed by the male heir of the second Earl. See Burke's *Vicissitudes of Families*, ii. 22.

in complexion, with a stately figure and an impressive and dignified bearing. He had the reputation of being in his day 'the ugliest man in England;' but his manner was happy and genial, his politeness true and genuine, and his address engaging, so that a general charm pervaded his features, and relieved them of the disqualification which nature had inflicted. In spite of his 'ugliness' he was a favourite subject of all the best artists of the day, and many portraits of him exist, painted by Reynolds, Gainsborough, Lawrence, &c.

In his personal relations with others he was generous and affable; in his domestic circle he was affectionate and warm-hearted. General Doyle, who served under him and who knew him well, makes the following comments upon his character[1]:—

'No man possessed in a higher degree the happy but rare faculty of attaching to him all who came within the sphere of his command. When they saw their general take upon himself the blame of any failure in the execution of his plans (provided it did not arise from want of zeal or courage), and where it succeeded giving the whole credit to those he employed, every man found himself safe; an unlimited confidence infused itself into all ranks, and his army became irresistible. Never was there a man of whom it could be more truly said, "Self was the only being seemed forgot!"'

The excess of his generosity, not unmixed with a fondness of display, led to unbounded extravagance, which, wasting a large private fortune, crippled his resources in his declining years. Nor is it impro-

[1] *Asiatic Journal*, (January 1827), xxiii. 6.

bable that his extraordinary attachment to the Prince of Wales did not a little contribute to the ruin of his affairs. 'Moira and I,' the Prince would sometimes say, 'are like two brothers, when one wants money he puts his hand in the other's pocket;' and to help his illustrious friend, he sold his estates in Ireland and much valuable property in England. Magnificent in his ideas, profuse in carrying them out, holding strongly to the old-fashioned notions of the obligation to serve those who from a high station had fallen into distress, he placed Donington Park at the disposal of the Bourbon princes when they emigrated to England during the French Revolution; and there they remained for several years. He received them with all the chivalrous consideration that their rank and misfortunes would naturally excite in the mind of a man of his character, and to supply their wants he opened his purse freely and gave them unlimited credit on his bankers; he accomplished this with much delicacy, for he left in each bedroom a signed cheque book, which the occupant could fill up at pleasure, without having to undergo the humiliation of asking for pecuniary assistance. It is only right to add that his guests availed themselves but sparingly of this generosity. His establishment in India was conducted with lavish expenditure, and when he returned home he prided himself on the fact that, after nine years' toil in the Eldorado of the East, he came back a poorer man than when he went out.

In short, he found himself in serious financial

embarrassments about this time, and in spite of a ruined constitution, and of increasing age and infirmities, he felt himself unable to enjoy that repose to which his career in India ought to have justly entitled him. He had to seek employment, and being offered the post of Governor and Commander-in-Chief in Malta, he accepted it in March 1824. There he devoted himself with his habitual energy to the affairs of the island, but soon his health gave way, and having fallen from his horse early in November, 1826, he sustained a serious injury to which he speedily succumbed. He was put on board H. M. S. Revenge, and was taken for a cruise in the Mediterranean; but he never rallied. After lingering a short time, showing great fortitude and resignation, he breathed his last, surrounded by his wife and four daughters, on the 28th of November, 1826, on board ship, in Baia Bay near Naples, in his seventy-second year. His body was brought to Malta and buried on the ramparts. He had desired that his right hand should be cut off and buried with his wife when she died; this wish was complied with, and now it rests clasped with hers in the family vault of the Loudouns at the old kirk of Loudoun, in Ayrshire.

When his grandson, the late Lord Hastings, well known in the racing world, died, the Marquessate and many of the other honours became extinct; but the Scotch Earldom of Loudoun and the old English Baronies descended to his grand-daughter, whose son, the present Lord Loudoun, represents the family.

We may conclude this chapter by the following passage from the pen of a contemporary writer:—

'To convey an adequate impression of the various qualities which adorned the Marquess of Hastings' private life and endeared him almost enthusiastically to every one who approached him nearly, would be a difficult task. His manners were peculiarly striking. The dignity of appearance, and the polished urbanity of his address, marked him at once as a gentleman of the highest order; but his good-breeding seemed the natural impulse of a kind disposition; and was as apparent in his intercourse with the humblest members of society as with persons of his own station. To those with whom he lived in habits of intimacy and friendship, he was not contented with rendering real service whenever the opportunity occurred; he never omitted those little attentions, the interchange of which constitutes so pleasing a part of private life. His mind was richly cultivated; his information was extensive, and at the same time minute; he was an excellent scholar, and was remarkable for the purity and elegance of his familiar language. His conversation was always interesting. . . . In addition to these qualities, he was blessed with the happiest temper, and possessed the warmest and most generous heart; and it may be truly said of him, that his ample fortune absolutely sank under the benevolence of his nature. He died with the most perfect resignation to the Divine Will, in charity with all mankind, and in those sentiments of elevated piety which had been habitual to his life[1].'

[1] *Annual Biography and Obituary*, xii. 157.

CHAPTER III

Condition of India in 1813

As the genius of Clive and the administrative reforms of his immediate successors consolidated the British possessions in Bengal, so did the rare intellectual power of Lord Wellesley create a system of imperial rule which, intimately connected with the events about to be recorded, became the basis of British supremacy in India. The causes which rendered the adoption of this system necessary cannot be described in this volume, for they belong to the period in which they arose; suffice it to say that the Marquess of Hastings (as we shall now call Lord Moira), though he resisted the views entertained by Wellesley when in England, recognised his mistake when he reached India, and became converted to the principles which he had previously denounced. His administration, in short, is the sequel to that of his illustrious predecessor; and hence in order to understand the questions which presented themselves to him when he landed at Calcutta in October, 1813, it is requisite to take a brief retrospective glance at Indian affairs, commencing some years before that date. It should however be stated at once, that the administrations of these two rulers, resembling each other in many ways, differed in one material respect, for while, in the earlier period, the ambition and power of the French was a disquieting element of no small magnitude, in that of Lord Hastings the danger had already passed away owing to the decline of Napoleon's ascendency, and the conquest in 1810 of Mauritius, which before that time had served as a base of naval operations against India.

Lord Wellesley found the sovereignty, which had fallen from the effete hands of the Mughal Emperors, contested by the Hindu or Maráthá confederacy of princes, and the various states governed by Muhammadan rulers. The latter were represented by the Nizám and by the Sultan of Mysore; the former consisted of five chiefs, at the head of which was the Peshwá of Poona, and under him, in a disorderly fashion, the Gáekwár of Baroda, Sindhia of Gwalior, and Holkar of Indore, both of whom ruled in Central India, and the Bhonsla Rájá of Nágpur, whose sway extended over Berar and Orissa.

Under the system inaugurated by the Governor-General, relations with the native states were regulated in the following manner. In the first place, there were those states with whom the British Government had concluded a subsidiary alliance. By this arrangement the princes concerned received a British force, called the '*subsidiary force*,' for the protection of the country, and they maintained a contingent of their own, sometimes commanded by European officers, to act with it;

they moreover agreed to pay for the maintenance of the subsidiary force, and nearly always ceded territory for the permanent discharge of this liability; and they also engaged to discontinue all political relations with other states, except in concert with the Government of Calcutta, and to submit all claims and disputes to its arbitration. The protected states were subject to a similar dependence, but their importance was not sufficiently great to oblige Government to maintain troops among them as was done elsewhere. And lastly came the princes whose independence was recognised, and with whom ordinary treaties—some of them more or less protective—were concluded.

Wellesley succeeded at first in putting an end so effectually to the aspirations of the Muhammadans, that during Lord Hastings' government little or no difficulty was experienced in that quarter. By these measures, the Nizám accepted a subsidiary alliance; the Karnátik was annexed; Mysore was reduced, the dynasty changed, and the state rendered dependent upon the British Government. Wellesley then turned his attention to the Maráthás, but they were engrossed in schemes of ambition, and were busy levying *chauth*, or 'quarter revenues,' beyond the limits of their own territories. Thus, enjoying a wild and unbridled license to plunder their own dominions and to harry their neighbours, they refused to agree to any terms. As a natural consequence of their own lawlessness they were quarrelling among themselves, and in the course of the struggle the Peshwá was defeated by

Holkar and fled for protection to British territory. Urged by his necessities, he signed a subsidiary treaty at Bassein, 1802; and thereupon threw consternation among the other confederates, who chafed to see their suzerain reduced by this act to a degrading position of dependence upon Calcutta. Hostilities followed in 1802–3, known as the second Maráthá war, and Sindhia and the Bhonsla Rájá were crushed. The power of these princes having been thus curtailed, and the Gaekwar having already accepted a subsidiary alliance, the only hostile Maráthá force left unsubdued was that of Holkar.

But the tide of victory had temporarily turned; the military operations which followed were not successful, disasters occurred, and Sindhia rose in revolt. Public opinion in England, moreover, dissatisfied with the vigour of Wellesley's Indian policy and failing to understand its importance, took alarm at these events and imagined that the solidity of British power was being overturned by a few freebooters. The result was that a great Anglo-Indian ruler was recalled before his work was concluded, and a successor appointed with instructions to reverse his system and to come to terms with the enemy at any price. Meanwhile the course of military events had again changed, and British arms were once more victorious; Holkar was flying before Lord Lake, and, as a matter of course, Sindhia promptly returned to his allegiance.

Peace was concluded at the end of 1805, but a

spirit of weak conciliation pervaded the negotiations and dictated the terms that were agreed upon; ill-timed concessions were granted, and these not only caused future embarrassments to the Government of Calcutta, but also pressed hardly upon the weaker states who had relied upon British support in moments of adversity. An example of this may be given, and is to be found in the dissolution of the protective alliance, 1806, with the Rájput principality of Jaipur, which was thus handed over to Maráthá and Pathán rapacity, under circumstances reflecting so little credit to English administration, that orders were issued in 1813 to reverse this act.

Lord Minto, who became Governor-General in 1807, found much to occupy him elsewhere, and had no leisure to devote to the affairs of Central India. The time and energies of his government were taken up in allaying discontent which had broken out in the Madras army, in carrying out foreign expeditions directed mainly against the French, and in establishing relations with distant Asiatic sovereigns with whom up to that time there had been little or no communication. The important internal questions had thus to be adjourned or temporarily adjusted. India was still much disturbed, but the Governor-General kept the Maráthás within certain bounds, without the necessity of war, and steered clear between a violation of the doctrine of non-intervention and a sacrifice of former prestige and of national interests[1].

[1] Sir W. Hunter's *Indian Empire, &c.*, Ed. 1882, p. 301.

The neutral policy adopted in England was founded upon a misconception, and it was held that India could be divided off into two sections—British and native—in the concerns of each of which the other was not to interfere. But it was forgotten that the two portions were indissolubly connected by ancient tradition and by geographical position, and Lord Minto was forced to show, in April, 1810, that the plan of preserving, or rather restoring, the balance of power—which it was supposed had been disturbed by territorial expansion—was an impossible proposition.

He declared that in India 'War, rapine, and conquest constitute an avowed principle of action, a just and legitimate pursuit, and the chief source of public glory, sanctioned and even recommended by the ordinances of religion, and prosecuted without the semblance or pretext of justice, with a savage disregard of every obligation of humanity and public faith, and restrained alone by the power of resistance.' After giving examples, he proceeded: 'It is unnecessary to refer to the testimony of specific facts, with a view to demonstrate the self-evident proposition, that the permanent existence of a balance of power is incompatible with reciprocal views of conquest and ambition;' and he wound up with 'this undeniable conclusion, that no extent of concession, or territorial restitution on our part, would have the effect of establishing any real and effectual balance of power in India, or forbearance on the part of other states, when the means of aggrandisement was placed in their hands[1].'

How far he would have succeeded in eradicating notions then prevalent, it is not easy to say, but the fact was becoming clearer every day that the settlement made in 1805 was far from satisfactory, more especially those treaties concluded with Sindhia and Holkar. These princes were military chiefs of irregular troops in the possession of a country, rather than territorial sovereigns; their dominion over their subjects was uncertain and precarious and was maintained by force, while their principal occupation was to levy, at the point of the sword, contributions and exactions from reluctant tributaries. The natural consequences followed, and there were perpetual scenes of war, anarchy, and bloodshed in those miserable states, disastrous to all prosperity, and dangerous to the neighbouring British provinces. In Holkar's territories disorder prevailed even to a greater extent than elsewhere, owing to the insanity of that prince in 1808 and to his death three years later; the young Holkar was a child, and his custody, and the power it conferred, was contested by his father's widow and by a soldier of fortune, Amír Khán, of whom more will be heard presently[2].

By Wellesley's plan of subsidiary alliances all

[1] General Sir John Malcolm's *Political History of India from 1784 to 1823*, 2 vols., London, 1826, vol. i. p. 430, &c. (hereafter quoted for brevity as Malcolm's *Hist. of India*).

[2] General Sir John Malcolm's *Memoir of Central India*, 3rd ed., 2 vols., London, 1832; vol. i. p. 260, &c.

these states would have been placed under civilised tutelage, the confusion which followed would have been minimised and gradually put an end to, and hence a more stable and worthy system of native rule would have been introduced. But the neutral policy of non-intervention had been accurately carried out, and Holkar, Sindhia, and the Bhonsla Rájá had been left independent in diminished territories, with the result that, deeply resenting their losses, they had free liberty, just outside British protection, to devastate what remained to them or what they could acquire from their neighbours, and to intensify the disorders which endangered the general tranquillity. In 1813 Holkar was unable to exercise much influence outside his own dominions, for reasons already given; but Sindhia and the Bhonsla Rájá were engaged in attacking Bhopál, an important little Muhammadan state connecting British territory in Bundelkhand and Berar, and governed by a Nawáb of superior political intelligence.

Lord Minto had been endeavouring since 1812 to induce the Bhonsla to accept a subsidiary alliance; but that prince, although saved from disaster at the hands of Amír Khán by a British force in 1809, brooded over the losses which he suffered in the last Maráthá war, and, forming schemes for his own aggrandisement, refused to alter the attitude of reserve and distrust which he persisted in maintaining towards the Government of Calcutta. Nor was the Peshwá inactive. He had claims on the

Gáekwár which were still unsettled, and which under the treaty of Bassein were controlled by the British authority; he resented this treaty and its consequences, and regretted his loss of influence; he was outwardly peaceable, but under this mask he was busily engaged in recovering his former ascendency over his confederates, in consolidating his power, and in secretly forming a powerful combination of native states to dispute British supremacy in the East. In short, among all the Maráthá chiefs there was, in 1813, a growing feeling that the time was approaching when they could avenge the past with impunity, drive the English out of India, and regain once more their ancient independence.

But there were two other powers, or rather associations, which played an important part in the events now under review. The Pindárís and the Patháns became a source of great danger, and their power to produce disorder, increasing in a very alarming manner between 1805 and 1813, is traceable to the settlement effected in the former year. The Pindárís[1] originally were Hindu outlaws who, frustrating the efforts of Aurangzeb to suppress them, added their strength to that of Sivají, the first Maráthá chief, who towards the end of the seventeenth century wrested power from the Mughals. As the Empire crumbled to pieces, so did they arise in fresh force, and,

[1] The word seems to occur first in 1689. Its derivation is uncertain; some think that it is connected with *Pandour*, but the Pindárís themselves trace it from *Pinda*, an intoxicating drink. Prinsep's *Transactions in India*, i. 37; Malcolm's *Central India*, i. 433.

degenerating into an organised banditti, became the terror and the scourge of the country which was submitted to their depredations. Owning no master, they attached themselves as irregular cavalry to the Peshwá's armies; but later they ranged themselves in two parties under Sindhia and Holkar, whom they adopted as patrons, though they continued to preserve their common traditions. They were accustomed to assemble every year about the beginning of November, and, having placed themselves under the bravest leaders, they sallied forth in mounted bands, often several thousand strong, to burn, destroy, and search for plunder. Nor were their raids conducted only in the neighbourhood of their camps, for such was the hardiness of their horses, the lightness of their baggage, and the rapidity of their movements, that they spread their devastations from Mysore northwards sometimes as far as the Jumna, and baffled the attempts of more regular forces to overtake them or keep them in check.

The centre of this formidable association was in the valley of the Narbadá, where the chiefs obtained lands, acquired small principalities, and were frequently honoured with the title of Nawáb. In 1814 they were reckoned at between 25,000 and 30,000 horsemen, of whom about half were well armed; their principal leaders were Chítu, Wasil Muhammad, and Kárím Khán—men who took a prominent part in the complicated and anarchical politics of Central India, now joining one faction and now another, but always pursuing their own selfish ends without thought of future consequences, and ever visiting with fire and sword the unfortunate people they plundered.

The Maráthá chiefs secretly favoured these predatory hordes, employing them often for their own purposes, and always disavowing responsibility when occasion required it; they never discouraged their increase, and, far from attempting to suppress the disorder, they made no effort even to mitigate it. When a Pindárí chief got too strong for them, they fomented the jealousies of a rival and sought to secure partial immunity for themselves by setting leader against leader; but the evil itself prospered and gained ground rapidly, and the settlement of 1805, far from putting an end to the troubles, such as they were in that year (as its advocates had hoped), only served to foster a most pernicious growth of marauders, by the independence which had been weakly conceded to the Maráthá princes at the end of a successful war.

It is obvious that the British Government was frequently harassed by these lawless bands, who, occupying a position nearly equidistant from the three Presidencies, moved readily in any direction from the centre of an extended circle, the circumference of which had constantly to be guarded. On two occasions considerable mischief had been done by them to British subjects or allies. In 1808–9 they entered Gujarát, and in 1812 they devastated Mirzápur and penetrated into territories which for years before had been free from their ravages. This last inroad into a British province was facilitated by the assistance of the Rájá of Rewá, a protected prince, and measures were in consequence taken against him, which were not concluded when Lord Hastings reached India.

The Patháns differed in some respects from the Pindárís; unlike the latter they were composed of paid troops who did not subsist on disorderly plunder, nor were they composed of cavalry only, but reckoned among their forces the most efficient native infantry then known in India which was not commanded by Europeans, as well as very useful artillery; they were therefore more regular in their habits and more disciplined in their demeanour than the Pindárís, banding themselves together in order to prey upon governments and princes, whereas the others ravaged defenceless villages and tortured the unfortunate inhabitants. But they resembled each other in being bodies of organised freebooters, without territorial relations and without responsible chiefs, who lived on rapine and disorder, and who caused serious trouble to the Government of Calcutta. Indeed the Patháns, and to a certain extent the Pindárís, were not unlike the Free Companies which in the Middle Ages overran parts of Europe, now enlisting as mercenaries under some prince, again fighting for their own hand and advantage, often plundering, and in every case oppressing both rulers and people. The Patháns devoted their energies more especially to Rájputána, and devastated that peculiarly disturbed collection of feudal states, where internal discord, hereditary quarrels, and continual strife made their career easy and prosperous. Amír Khán was the most successful Patháh leader, and had under him an army of some 30,000 men; he might indeed, like another Sforza, have carved out for himself an important principality in those troublous times, had his abilities been sufficient for the purpose, and had his ambition lain in that direction; but he preferred the wild and exciting life of a captain of Condottieri, and as such made an excellent living out of the feuds he fomented and the disorder he created.

The great central tract of the Indian continent presented truly a pitiable spectacle, and never before had there been such intense and general suffering. The native states were disorganised and society on the very verge of dissolution; the people were crushed by despots and ruined by exactions; the country was overrun by bandits and its resources wasted by enemies; armed forces existed only to plunder, to torture, and to mutiny; briefly, government there was none, it had ceased to exist, there remained only misery and oppression [1].

Besides this serious condition of affairs, Lord Hastings found on reaching Calcutta in 1813 that there was another question of moment which required

[1] H. T. Prinsep's *History of the Political and Military Transactions in India during the Administration of the Marquess of Hastings*, 1813–1823, 2 vols., London, 1825, i. chap. i; H. H. Wilson's Edition of Mill's *History of British India*, London, 1846, viii. 181; Malcolm's *Central India*, i. 325, 426.

his attention, and to this we must now revert. Nepál is a long and narrow mountainous region, in appearance like a band of ribbon, of uniform breadth, stretching from the plains of Hindustán to the high lands of Tibet, some 700 miles long by 100 broad. On the north it is bounded by the Himálayas, on the south by Delhi, Rohilkhand, Oudh, and the Bengal provinces, and on the east and west by the Tistá river and the Sutlej respectively. Nepál was always outside the pale of the Mughal Empire; but as it forms the upper fringe of the northern basin of the Ganges, with no natural barrier on the south, its geographical position is important and connects it closely with the territories in English possession.

The original inhabitants were of Tibetan stock, among whom Hindu colonists settled, led it is supposed by Rájput chieftains who established themselves as petty independent Rájás over the country. There was perpetual war and perennial anarchy, until a mountain tribe, called the Gúrkhas, overran in 1767 the valley of Khátmándu, and gradually extended their conquests over the whole region known as Nepál. The Gúrkhas claimed to be of Rajput descent; they were organised on a military and feudal basis, with an army trained on the English model, and were far superior in national discipline and in political intelligence to the races they conquered. In less than fifty years they acquired and consolidated supreme power, gave their name to the whole country, and, notwithstanding internal commotions, prosecuted their foreign wars with unabated energy. It was therefore only natural that so warlike and aggressive a people should endeavour to push into the plains and thus come in contact with the British power. Frequent encroachments on the part of these mountaineers took place even in the last century, and these led to protests and to reprisals, but not, until Lord Hastings' time, to actual war[1].

The immediate cause of dispute arose through the treaty of Lucknow, 1801, under which portions of the possessions of the Nawáb Wazír of Oudh were ceded to the British Government, in lieu of a large sum of money due from that prince. Gorakhpur, a part of these territories, bordered upon Nepál, and on this frontier there were frequent quarrels, which had continued from time immemorial, between the petty Rájás owning the rich plains and the valuable forests beyond, and those who lived in the hills; as a consequence of numerous raids and counter-raids, several chieftains held lands both in Nepál and in Hindustán. Now the English, on acquiring a province, left all existing rights intact; but the Gúrkhas, on conquering a district, dispossessed the Rájás of their territories and secured them for themselves; hence they asserted and vindicated claims on lands in Bengal which were held by chiefs they had ousted from Nepál. Two cases of dispute became prominent during the administration of Sir George Barlow: one, in which the Nepalese

[1] Wilson's *Hist. of British India*, viii. 4 (title set forth in full in foot-note, *ante*, p. 55; and hereafter quoted for brevity as *Wilson*).

seized a British fief, called Batwál, held by a hill Rájá whose property had been confiscated by them; and another where a district, Seoráj, was retained by them, on the ground that they had possession of it when the treaty of Lucknow was signed. Sir G. Barlow, while protesting against both these acts, proposed that Batwál should be evacuated and Seoráj assigned to the Gúrkhas; but the affair was not pursued further, and the Nepalese remained in occupation until 1810–11, when they made further encroachments from both these places and advanced into another British fief in the district of Sarán.

The Indian Government observing that a gradual invasion was being persistently made into the all-important valley of the Ganges, now endeavoured to regulate the frontier, and early in 1812 Lord Minto offered to do so on the basis of compromise which had been proposed by his predecessor; but he received for reply that the Nepalese were in their rights and had not yet occupied all that was due to them. Commissioners from both sides, however, were at last assembled for a judicial investigation of the various claims which had been set up, and upon examination it became apparent that the Gúrkhas had no vestige of a right to any of the fiefs they had seized; a demand was therefore made in 1813 for their evacuation, but as the demand was evaded, Lord Minto addressed in June a formal letter to the Gúrkha government calling upon the latter in conciliatory terms to redress the frontier disputes. The answer did not arrive until

Lord Hastings had assumed control of Indian affairs, but it was evident, from what had already passed, that force would have to be employed if the question was to be settled. For a long time the Gúrkhas had been unmolested, and in spite of frequent remonstrances they were approaching little by little within a perilous proximity to the centre of the Bengal provinces; it was therefore necessary to arrest this invasion, which, far from being confined to two or three points, had been allowed to menace the whole length of the frontier[1].

To sum up:—the area of British influence in India had advanced with gigantic strides in fifty years. It extended not only over the lands in actual possession, but over those also where subsidiary treaties of alliance and protection existed. The friendly native princes were held to the Government of Calcutta by ties of interest and duty, and had acquired thereby a new position which had to be respected and definite rights which had to be maintained. A powerful confederation was being established and a vast Empire was in process of consolidation,—fixed on a firm foundation and supplanting that of the Mughals,—at the head of which stood England as Suzerain, and grouped around her, great native feudatories, whose peaceable development she was bound to foster and whose national independence she had to preserve. The

[1] Prinsep's *Transactions* (title set forth in full in footnote, *ante*, p. 55; and hereafter quoted for brevity as *Prinsep*), vol. i. pp. 54, 78.

north-west of the Indian continent beyond the Sutlej river was, in 1813, outside the pale of her direct activity, but the sphere of her responsibility spread through more than half the remainder; that is to say, it extended roughly speaking over the whole of Hindustán, except where a huge double wedge of territory was driven into the centre of the Empire and separated the Presidency of Bombay from the remainder.

This wedge divided Delhi from Baroda, and formed on the one side an immense irregular triangle whose apex was south of Nágpur near the Godávari river, and on the other side an elongated figure running south as far as Mysore and lying between the sea and the Nizám's dominions of Haidarábád. This alien territory occasioned extensive frontiers, which were not easily guarded, and made communications difficult, sometimes impossible, between the various portions of the growing Empire. But in addition, the independent portion of India was in a state bordering on chaos, and was in close proximity and in intimate relations with states only recently absorbed into the British confederation. Anarchy is always contagious, and a danger had thus arisen which it was time to remove. To effect this, and to settle this immense tract of country, was the great and primary problem that was to occupy Lord Hastings, and his course of action in the matter forms the central object of interest of his administration.

But on assuming control of affairs, he found himself

entangled by another and a troublesome question which required adjustment. He had here to deal with a disciplined and brave nation of mountaineers who threatened to make a descent upon the provinces lying close to the very seat of Empire. This nation, composed of men inured to hardships and trained to conquer, might easily arrest the schemes which were being formed for the thorough pacification of India; and hence the questions involved could not be adjourned and had to be dealt with at once.

Of minor problems there were of course many, and without counting those of greater importance which have already been alluded to, Lord Hastings says that he began his term of office with no less than five 'hostile discussions with native powers, each capable of entailing resort to arms.' Of these, four were amicably adjusted, and the fifth (the dispute with the Rájá of Rewá) was settled by a successful attack upon one of the strongholds of that prince. But in addition to all this, there were serious financial embarrassments to be faced, which threatened to interfere with the great work to be done in Central India. The resources of Bengal were running low, and the treasuries in the three Presidencies were nearly exhausted; there was and there had been a demand for money at home, and this demand had to be supplied; the rate of exchange was against India, and it was difficult to raise a loan. Economy had therefore been practised, and the military establishments had been reduced in a manner that alarmed the authorities in India. But financial difficulties, though they hamper, never baffle the plans of an energetic administrator, and despite the serious inconveniences felt at the moment, they proved to be temporary only, and the business of government was carried on with vigour and success[1].

[1] Wilson, viii. 3; Prinsep, i. 215; Summary of the Administration of the Indian Government, from October, 1813, to January, 1823, by the Marquess of Hastings, Governor-General, London, 1824 (published in *The Pamphleteer*, London, vol. xxiv), p. 3, &c.

CHAPTER IV

THE STORY OF A TREATY. THE GÚRKHA WAR, 1814–16

It has already been said that affairs in Nepál claimed Lord Hastings' first attention, and the preliminary proceedings connected therewith have just been related. In December, 1813, on receipt of an unsatisfactory answer to the representations made to the Gúrkha government in the previous June, the Governor-General replied by peremptorily demanding the evacuation of the districts where encroachments had been made, and, according to precedent, ordered the local magistrate to occupy them if they were not given up in twenty-five days. After the prescribed delay this order was carried out, and the Gúrkhas retired without making the least resistance: it was then supposed that the incident was at an end, and police posts were established, the troops being withdrawn. But it was far otherwise; the Nepalese had determined upon war, though some of the wisest chiefs were opposed to it, and in May they surprised the occupied districts and drove out the police. Lord Hastings now resolved to settle once for all these border disputes, which constituted a danger along the whole frontier, especially to Bengal, and after mature consideration, decided to take the offensive; but he also gave his adversary time for reflection, and did not sign the proclamation which explained the causes of the war till the 1st November[1].

His plan was to invade Nepál by four columns, from two directions. In the west, General Ochterlony (6,000 native troops and 16 guns) was ordered to operate in the hilly country near the Sutlej; and on his right General Gillespie (1,000 Europeans, 2,500 natives, and 11 guns) was to push from Meerut to the lower spurs of the mountains, between the upper Ganges and Jumna, and detaching a force against Srínagar, to incline to the left and support the first column. In the east, General J. S. Wood (1,000 Europeans, 3,000 natives, and 11 guns) was to penetrate into Palpa from Gorakhpur, and to co-operate with the main body under General Marley (1,000 Europeans, 7,000 natives, and 26 guns), who was to advance from Patná upon the capital Khátmándu. Besides, local troops were placed in position to defend the rest of the frontier, and a force of 2,000 men was formed under Major Latter, to operate defensively towards Sikkim and to support the Rájá of that district against the Gúrkhas. Lord Hastings, who had made these dispositions, directed the operations from Lucknow.

To resist this attack, the Gúrkhas had no more than

[1] This proclamation, dated from Lucknow, is printed in full in Malcolm's *Hist. of India*, Appendix vii.

12,000 regular troops and some raw levies imperfectly armed and not always well-affected to their rulers. But the invaders had no easy task to perform. The Indian forces were to advance through a rugged and impracticable region full of defensive defiles, the geography of which was unknown; they had had no experience in mountain operations, and were not trained to the difficulties it entails; and their opponents were a warlike people, who were ready to take intelligent advantage of every military position in their native hills, and who had occupied and fortified all the passes that led into the country.

The campaign opened badly, even disastrously. The two columns in the west advanced, middle of October, and were opposed to Amar Singh, who had only 4000 men under his command; General Ochterlony it is true penetrated by paths 'indescribably bad,' and almost impassable, as far as Bilåspur, forcing the local Rájá to submit and turning the enemy's position at Arki, but these partial successes were as nothing when compared with the serious reverses experienced by Gillespie's division. The progress of that column was soon arrested by one hill fort, Kalanga or Nalápáni, garrisoned by a mere handful of the enemy, and two assaults were beaten back, the British general was killed, and more than 500 of his men were lost; after a month's delay, it seemed to dawn upon the invaders that the Gúrkhas might be shelled out of the fort, and as there was no bomb-proof cover in Kalanga, the place was at last reduced with ease, and without any further loss, 30th

November. A strong detachment was then left in the neighbourhood[1], (the advance on Srínagar being given up), and the remainder now pushed towards Ochterlony; but on attempting to assault Jaitak, the attacking columns did not come up at the proper time, and being beaten in detail, they were again repulsed with great loss. Nor did the British troops operating in the east improve the fortunes of the war; Wood's division received a slight check before a stockade, and the commander, believing exaggerated accounts of the enemy's strength, pleaded that he was too weak to advance any further. General Marley also accomplished absolutely nothing; but two of his detached posts of 500 men each, which had been left without sufficient support, were surprised and cut to pieces. As a small compensation for the failures in this quarter, however, a portion of the plains of the Tarái was occupied, and the co-operation of the Sikkim Rájá was secured.

This was the state of affairs in the end of January 1815. Up to that date everything had failed, and the Gúrkhas, elated by their victories, still held the passes and defied the numerous forces brought against them. The British had lost heavily; they were obliged to draw upon

[1] This detachment commanded the lines of communication between the western and eastern portions of Nepál, and was instrumental in capturing part of Amar Singh's correspondence. It appeared thereby that this chief had opposed the war from the beginning, as incurring a grave risk without necessity, and that he also opposed those who wanted to make terms when the Gúrkhas were in difficulties. Some of this interesting correspondence is printed in Prinsep's *Transactions*, i. 457 and 462.

their resources, and drain the garrisons of all available troops, to fill up the gaps occasioned by the disasters, and to supply the unexpected requirements which so serious a mountain campaign had entailed. Reinforcements were sent without stint to the eastern theatre of operations; but notwithstanding every effort made by Lord Hastings to urge an advance towards Khátmándu, the commanders remained inactive and could not be induced to enter the hills. 12,000 men were also pushed as rapidly as possible to the western divisions, where operations were prudently and energetically pursued, and there eventually victory dawned once more upon the British standards.

Meanwhile the worst effect had been produced in Central India by the war; the Maráthá princes began to realise that the English had suffered a severe repulse; they imagined that the moment was approaching when they could assume the offensive; communications to this end were going on between the native courts, and between the latter and the Gúrkhas; Amír Khán, the Pathán chief, showed signs of activity, and Ranjít Singh, the celebrated ruler of the Sikhs, was collecting an army at Lahore. Before the war, the Governor-General, having determined that the Pindárís should not repeat their raids into territory under his rule or protection, had already made effective provision against such a calamity; but at this juncture these precautions had to be redoubled, and a warlike attitude assumed in other directions as well as towards the north. The dangers that menaced the British

Government at this critical moment caused deep anxiety. Amír Khán, only twelve marches from Delhi, was supposed to have in his camp 30,000 fighting men of good quality, and 125 guns; he maintained his troops with difficulty when constrained to be inactive, and he was waiting in the 'hope of untoward events occurring to us in the Nepalese war,—an expectation founded on the extravagant opinion entertained of the Gúrkha power, and on the distorted accounts circulated respecting the reverses we had already suffered in the contest.' Lord Hastings had 4500 cavalry and infantry to resist this threatened invasion, and he meant to put himself at their head should occasion require it. A force of 1000 irregular horse was held in hand to oppose the Pindárís. The troops, moreover, at Cawnpur were left there for the purpose of keeping Sindhia in check, who was at Gwalior, only three marches from the Doáb, five from Delhi, and five from Agra[1].

Failure and danger did not discourage the Governor-General; he sought for fresh means to reduce the enemy and, as will be seen, speedily found them; he set himself vigorously to grapple with the difficulties of the moment, and was all the more determined to bring the war to a successful termination. He attributed the checks which the British arms had experi-

[1] The Private Journal of the Marquess of Hastings, K.G., Governor-General and Commander in Chief in India, Edited by his daughter, the Marchioness of Bute, 2 vols., London 1858, i. 296. (Hereafter quoted for brevity as *Private Journal.*)

enced to their proper causes,—in the eastern theatre of operations to inactivity and incapacity, and in the western to imprudence and rashness. Knowing that the Company's armies had never before had to contend against a foe like the Gúrkhas, he had been specially careful to provide for contingencies, which his more varied experience in the field had taught him were only too likely to arise in a mountain warfare, directed against so formidable an enemy as the Nepalese.

'The mischief which had occurred from inconsiderate attempts to storm places by no means calculated to be carried in that manner, had made me insert as an article in the instructions to each of the generals commanding divisions, a special prohibition against that species of attack upon any works which should be of a quality to require artillery for their reduction. When Colonel Mawbey was to be dispatched against Kalanga, Major-General Gillespie was directed by me to enforce upon Colonel Mawbey's mind a strict attention to the above injunction. I received from Major-General Gillespie an answer, saying that he had impressed strongly on Colonel Mawbey the caution dictated by me. Colonel Mawbey, in consequence, on reconnoitring the place forebore to assault it, and reported to Major-General Gillespie that he meant to establish batteries against it, as he conceived it was impossible to carry it by storm. The Major-General on this quitted his own column, repaired to the camp before Kalanga, and on examining the fortress resolved to assault it. The result was the only one that could be rationally expected. The discredit to our arms, and the baneful influence which this reverse must have upon future operations, are light in comparison to the loss of Major-General Gillespie. Whatsoever was the indiscretion of this last step, it cannot detract from the credit due to the many important services achieved by his heroic valour. His zeal, his energy, and his resources rendered him infinitely material for the conduct of operations in a country the features of which are so novel to officers accustomed to the plains of Hindustán. Genius like his would soon have fashioned others to a just conception of the system to be pursued in mountain warfare; and, deprived of him, I fear they will have to poke their way amid many errors and oversights before they attain such experience as may give them due confidence in themselves [1].'

Animated by such generous sentiments towards a commander, whose indiscretion had led to serious disaster, the Governor-General was not long in reviving the *morale* of his army, where the generals did their duty, and there the troops were not disheartened. Reverses only stimulated them to greater exertions, taught them how to operate in the mountains and to avoid the dangers they presented, and made them imitate the tactics of the enemy, by establishing defensive posts for their better security. Fortune moreover favoured Lord Hastings. Bitter dissensions raged among the Pindárís and prevented them from acting together; Ranjít Singh was threatened by an invasion by the Amír of Kábul and was forced to look after his own affairs, and Sindhia's commanders came to an open rupture and fought among themselves. The danger of an anti-British combination began to disperse, and a decided advantage was soon obtained by

[1] Private Journal, i. 223.

the next step which the Commander-in-Chief took to subjugate the Nepalese.

The two theatres of the war, on the Sutlej and near the Gandak river, were 400 miles apart, and the Nepalese province of Kumáun, lying between the two and bordering upon Rohilkhand, was untouched by the hostilities, and was almost unoccupied by the enemy. Lord Hastings perceived that an attack upon this province would not only divert the attention of the Gúrkhas from the flanks of their kingdom, but that, owing to its peculiar geographical formation, an expedition there, if successful, would also cut the country in two, and absolutely isolate Amar Singh; moreover, knowing that the people of Kumáun were disaffected towards their rulers, he determined to carry the war into that province. Being short of troops he raised levies among the Rohillás, and selected two officers to command them, Colonel Gardner and Major Hearsey, who, previous to 1802, had served in the Maráthá forces. These irregular bodies of troops advanced almost simultaneously early in February.

Gardner, aware that his Rohillás could not resist the Gúrkhas in open fight, pushed up the Kosi river, and evading a serious engagement, marched round the enemy's flank: after a series of brilliant manœuvres on their communications, he forced them (28th March) to retire to Almora, the capital of the province, where he followed them, and prepared for future operations. Hearsey proceeded up the river Kálí, and at first met with no resistance, but on marching towards his colleague, he found the way blocked by a hill fort, before which he had to spend the month of March in trying to reduce it.

Lord Hastings, who was all this time directing every military movement from a distance, and who had full knowledge of political events, found that the dangers to be apprehended in Central India in January had now passed away; he accordingly ordered up a force of 2500 men with 10 guns, under Colonel Nicholls, 23rd March, to the support of Gardner's irregulars. The junction between these two bodies was effected early in April, and it was not a day too soon, for Hearsey got into difficulties that might have brought ruin on the whole expedition.

The Gúrkha government finding that they were not pressed in the eastern theatre, and having heard of the Rohillá invasion as well as the necessities of Amar Singh (who as will be seen presently was at this time harassed by Ochterlony), now dispatched a body of troops across the Kálí to ward off the danger that threatened them. This force defeated Hearsey, and not only took him prisoner, but recovered all his posts, and overran the country he had conquered. Flushed with this success, the Gúrkhas marched to Almora, and reached that town a day or two after Nicholls had joined Gardner. They now endeavoured to manœuvre against the British, but on the 23rd April they were defeated and their commander killed, and two days later an outwork of the town was assaulted and carried. The enemy, though much pressed in consequence of this misfortune, defended themselves gallantly to the last, and made a spirited night attack; but after a very severe fight they were again repulsed with loss, and the next day guns were brought to bear at a close range upon the town itself. Finding all further resistance useless, the Gúrkha commander proposed to treat, and a convention was agreed to, 27th April 1815, by which the whole province of Kumáun with all its strongholds were surrendered, and the Gúrkha troops removed to the east of the Kálí river.

General Martindell, who succeeded Gillespie in the command of the second division, which had already suffered considerably, did not again move against Jaitak till the 12th February; after fighting some skirmishes with varying fortune, and laboriously overcoming the physical difficulties of getting heavy guns into almost inaccessible positions, he levelled the enemy's stockades to the ground by artillery fire, 20th March; but having accomplished so much, he now unaccountably came to the conclusion that it would be unsafe to assault the open town, though his forces were double the number of those of his opponents, and he preferred to blockade them and reduce the place by starvation. The investment of Jaitak was completed in the middle of April, in the course of which several actions took place, where the British were uniformly successful; but the process adopted was a lengthy one, and Martindell's plan did not secure the capitulation of the stronghold.

By the end of March, all the forts that were besieged in the rear of General Ochterlony's advance to Bilâspur were reduced and occupied, and his communications being now clear, he was prepared to take another step forward. Amar Singh stood in the way and occupied a strong fortified position in the mountains near where Simla is now situated, and there Ochterlony determined to attack him, on 14th April. This position having been carefully reconnoitred, it was found that there were two important points in it which were left unfortified and insufficiently held by the enemy. A night attack was undertaken, and while the Gúrkhas were amused by feints, the two points were quickly seized and strengthened. It was now, though too late, apparent to the Gúrkhas that they had been outmanœuvred, and that they must either endeavour to recover these places, or submit to have their whole defensive line broken and rendered useless. Adopting the former course they hurled themselves, 2000 strong, desperately and with their wonted valour and fury, against the British troops who had surprised them, and on the 16th fought one of the most severely contested battles of the whole war: but the struggle did not last long; soon their ardour began to slacken, and then, a counter-attack being made, they were put to flight with a loss of 500 men. The English general immediately pressed forward, and brought up the remainder of his men to close upon Maláun, the principal work of the enemy's position; early in May a battery was raised against it, and about the same time, the news of the fall of Almora having reached the Gúrkha camp, Amar Singh was deserted by the largest part of his forces. But it was not till a breach had been made in the walls of the fort, on 15th May, that this brave old chief would consent to sign a capitulation. By the convention then agreed upon, the Gúrkhas retired to the east of the Kálí river, and the whole of the Nepalese territory to the west was surrendered to the English; Jaitak capitulated under this convention.

The western portion of Nepál, a territory more than 200 miles in length, was thus occupied by these successful operations, and immediate arrangements were made for its settlement. The province of Kumáun was taken over and administered by the Government of Calcutta, but the remainder of the conquered tract of country was handed over to the native Rájás whom Amar Singh had dispossessed; the general principle which guided the British authorities being, to leave as much as possible of these districts in the same condition as they had been prior to the Gúrkha invasion, practically free and independent, but subject to control and protection from Calcutta in case of internal disorders or foreign disputes. Many of the Gúrkha troops also who had fought so gallantly against the British, were, owing to the convention, disbanded, and some of them were allowed to take service under their former adversaries; in this way three battalions were formed from this excellent military material. The season for active operations in the field had now passed away, and there was a lull in the war lasting over the summer months. During this time, preparations were made for a renewal of hostilities. The forces in the eastern theatre were reinforced, and a brigade was formed on the Kálí and put under Colonel Adams, the former commander in this quarter, Colonel Nicholls, relieving General Wood on the frontier near Palpa; while General Ochterlony, having been withdrawn from the west, assumed command of the main force destined to march upon Khátmándu.

It was only natural that the Gúrkha government should seek for peace after the disasters to which they had been subjected, and the summer of 1815 was accordingly devoted to negotiations to this purpose. The following were the terms offered by the Marquess of Hastings:—

1. Cession of the conquered country from the Sutlej to the Kálí river, and of the whole of the Tarái, or the fertile plains skirting the southern limits of Nepál and extending from the upper Ganges to the Tistá river;

2. Independence of the Sikkim Rájá; and

3. Acceptance of a Resident at the court of Khátmándu.

These terms were rejected, but it was ascertained that the only point which was a real obstacle to a settlement on the above basis was the cession of the Tarái, the court of Khátmándu being ready to give up those portions which were claimed as British territory, but not where the authority of Nepál had always been acknowledged. Lord Hastings being aware of the importance of these plains to the Gúrkhas, now drafted a treaty by which the cession of the Tarái from the Kálí to the Gandak river was insisted upon, and of the remainder, only so much as the British troops occupied, offering at the same time an annual subsidy of two lakhs of rupees, as a compensation for the loss incurred. He was the more anxious to come to terms with the Rájá of Khátmándu, since extension of territory had formed no part of his object, and the war had only been undertaken in order to put an end for ever to Nepalese aggressions and to secure permanently and securely the northern frontiers of the Empire. This draft treaty was declared to be final and to contain the utmost concessions that could be granted; it was then delivered to the Gúrkha envoy, who, not venturing to sign it of his own authority, returned with it to his court and promised to bring back an answer; he reappeared on the 28th November, and signed the draft treaty at Segauli on that date.

Meanwhile Lord Hastings had taken into account the protracted nature of these negotiations and had observed the repugnance which the clause relating to the Tarái had excited in the minds of the Gúrkhas; desiring moreover that all future causes of misunderstanding should be avoided, and in order to cement a friendship with a brave people whose good will he hoped to obtain, he still endeavoured to make them some gratuitous concessions. The treaty was ratified by the Supreme Government of Calcutta on the 9th December, and the latter awaited this necessary formality from Khátmándu (which was promised on the 15th), to give effect to the conciliatory views which were then to be put into practice.

But the war faction was again in the ascendent in the Rájá's councils. This faction—holding exaggerated opinions of the value of the fortified passes which, guarding the capital, had never yet been approached by the British forces, apprehensive, moreover, lest the proposed peace should result in the complete overthrow of the Gúrkha state and reduce it to a position of dependence and servitude, and having already surrendered the western provinces without hope or means of recovering them—conceived that they had nothing more to lose and much to gain by a renewal of hostilities, and accordingly the ratification of the treaty was rejected, to the extreme astonishment and annoyance of the British authorities. As soon as this became evident, General Ochterlony was forthwith ordered to take the field and a second campaign became inevitable.

Some delay at first occurred owing to the fact that peace was looked upon as certain, and that a spirit of hasty economy had induced the authorities to sell off a large quantity of stores, transport, and other warlike necessaries; it was not therefore until the beginning of February, 1816, that an advance was made into the enemy's country. A large force of nearly 20,000 men, including three European regiments, was by this time collected and divided into four strong brigades, of which one on the right was directed upon Hariharpur, another on the left up the Gandak to Rámnagar, and the remainder, the main body under the general himself, moved straight up the road to Khátmándu. On the 10th the latter force reached the entrance of the pass and there found the enemy strongly entrenched behind a triple line of fortification, which being reconnoitred was judged to be too strong to be taken by a direct attack. But the Gúrkhas contented themselves with a mere passive defence, and remained quiescent behind their stockades; thus the invaders were enabled on the 14th to proceed up an unguarded path and turn these formidable defences.

A brigade started at night on this perilous march, led by General Ochterlony, unaccompanied even by a solitary baggage animal; they struggled along slowly and laboriously in single file, through deep and rocky defiles, across sombre and tangled forests, and up rugged and precipitous ascents; but after lengthened toil and numerous difficulties, their efforts were amply rewarded, for the next day they reached and occupied a position in rear of the enemy's defences; and the Gúrkhas surprised and almost surrounded were obliged hurriedly to evacuate all their works, and to retreat precipitately to the north without even striking a blow.

Pressing on as rapidly as possible, the two brigades of the central column formed a junction on the banks of the river Rapti, and having established a depôt, Ochterlony came up with the enemy at Magwampar, about 20 miles from Khátmándu, and seized a village on the right of their position. The Gúrkhas observing their danger in this quarter, attempted to retake the village, and according to their usual practice in such an emergency, charged it furiously with 2000 men, the bulk of their forces; but in vain, for supports were moved forward, and they were repulsed and driven back within their stockades, leaving some guns and more than 800 men on the field, (28th). Next day the left brigade, which had advanced by Rámnagar, joined the main body, having reached the valley of the Rapti almost without opposition and having secured its rear. The right brigade had been slightly delayed in its advance on Hariharpur, by the difficulties of the ground, but on the 1st March this position was successfully turned and an attack of the Gúrkhas was defeated with great loss; the same night Hariharpur was evacuated and the next day it was converted into a depôt; the brigade was about to advance, when the commander received an intimation that the war was over.

The success and the rapidity of General Ochterlony's operations had at last entirely removed the delusion under which the court of Nepál had laboured. The mountain passes had been proved to be useless, they were turned with ease by British valour, the capital lay open to assault, and dismay reigned supreme at the unexpected result. The official Red Seal of the

Gúrkhas was now affixed in haste to the treaty of Segauli, and dispatched at once to the English camp, with a humble petition that it might be accepted and the past forgotten. General Ochterlony, aware that the unhealthy season was approaching in which it would not be easy to maintain an army in the seat of war, and being fully empowered to do so, received the Nepalese envoy and concluded the treaty; not however before the Gúrkhas had made ample submission and had ceded all territory up to the Rapti, which was now constituted as the new frontier.

Thus at last was peace made, after many incidents, disappointments, and successes, and the crushed Nepalese evinced much alacrity to perform its conditions. Lord Hastings, seeing that they were duly humbled and knowing that victory placed him above the suspicion of weakness, could now afford to be generous; he therefore gave effect to the conciliatory policy which he conceived would produce a lasting friendship between Calcutta and Khátmándu. These final arrangements were made later, and a frontier was traced out and marked by pillars of masonry; the English, in lieu of the annual subsidy of two lakhs of rupees, gave back to Nepál the Tarái, and only retained such parts as were necessary to rectify the border line; but a small strip of these plains was also handed over to the Rájá of Sikkim—with whom a protective treaty was signed February, 1817; moreover, as the Nawab Wazír of Oudh had relieved the Governor-General from serious financial embarrassments during the contest, and had advanced two crores of rupees for the maintenance of the war, the Tarái which skirted that prince's territory was retained and was given to him, in payment of half the debt so incurred.

The treaty of Segauli [1], as modified by the arrangements just mentioned, defines British relations with Nepál ever since that time, and the peaceable attitude maintained by that nation towards the Indian Government furnishes the best proof of the moderation and the wisdom which formulated its provisions. These provisions, having already been stated, need not be further alluded to here; it is sufficient to say that they gradually effected the purpose for which they were intended. As a result of the war, all danger for the northern frontier has been happily removed for ever; irritating questions with a neighbour, powerful for evil in moments of adversity, have been definitely settled; and the best fighting material that India affords has been enlisted, and has proved its valour, in the defence of British supremacy in that continent.

It may be interesting to observe here, that the Chinese interposed in the arrangements made with Nepál. The Celestial Empire exercised a sort of suzerainty over the country, and when everything was well over, wanted to know (end of 1816) what the struggle was all about. A correspondence took place between Calcutta and Pekin on the subject, when the Chinese authorities declared themselves

[1] The text of this Treaty is given in Prinsep's *Transactions*, i. 473.

satisfied, but hinted that the Resident should be removed from Khátmándu. The Governor-General, however, informed them that at least one civilised nation ought to be represented at that capital, and ingeniously suggested that a mandarin would suit his purpose equally well,—an inadmissible proposal, as he knew well, seeing that the Chinese government was too exalted an authority then to condescend to foreign missions [1].

The news of the Gúrkha war was at first received with unmitigated regret in England. The Charter of 1813 had thrown open the Indian trade, and had destroyed the Company's monopoly, and it had been hoped that the use of money might partially serve to nullify this obnoxious enactment. Many members of the Court of Directors resented the diversion of these funds to a military expedition, and appeared even to think that a war which had become supremely necessary must be neglected because it interfered with a commercial speculation. The Court, indeed, did not propose that the Governor-General should submit tamely to unjust encroachment; but, failing to understand the temper of the Gúrkha chiefs, they hoped that as the result of local investigation had established 'the Company's right to the disputed lands, the government of Nepál would yield to the application for the surrender of those lands' without the display of force. But Lord Hastings, knowing well that everything short of war had been tried *ad nauseam*,

[1] Wilson, viii. 79.

without success, exhibited little patience with such vacillation, and trenchantly remarked:—

'I certainly had an option; I might shrink from the declaration plighted by Lord Minto, abandoning the property of the Company, sacrificing the safety of our subjects, and staining the character of our government, or I had to act up to the engagements bequeathed to me, and to reprove the trespass of an insatiable neighbour. That I should have chosen the latter alternative will hardly afford ground for censure[1].'

It is unnecessary to dwell upon the criticisms made by the Court of Directors on the dispositions for the war planned by the Governor-General,—at one time advocating defensive operations (the futility of which had been amply demonstrated by Generals Wood and Marley early in 1815), and again a concentration of forces (neglecting local circumstances which made the opposite course the most judicious),—it is more satisfactory to observe that at the termination of the war, the Court with generous unanimity bestowed praise and thanks upon the Governor-General and the gallant General Ochterlony, who had both of them fulfilled their difficult tasks with such conspicuous success and with such advantage to the best interests of India[2].

[1] Wilson, viii. 76.

[2] It was upon this occasion that Lord Moira was created Marquess of Hastings, and at the same time General Ochterlony, who had previously been made a K.C.B., was also created a Baronet.

CHAPTER V

The Gathering of the Storm. Events in Central India, 1814–16

It was not long before Lord Hastings became impressed with the lawlessness which prevailed in Central India, and early in 1814 he made strong representations to the home authorities on the subject; but meanwhile he neglected no precaution calculated to maintain peace in British territory, and with this object he considered two courses which seemed to be open to him. A subsidiary treaty with the Bhonsla Rájá of Nágpur presented the best advantages, as thereby a secure central position would be acquired, communications between Bundelkhand and Haidarábád strengthened, and a great length of frontier defended. But the old negotiations which had been begun with that ruler in 1812, on being revived, failed in 1814, and nothing more for the present was to be expected in that quarter. The other plan was to connect the north and the south by a line of friendly native states, of which Bhopál was the most important; and here circumstances contributed to render the realisation of this course probable.

Bhopál had been seriously threatened by Sindhia and the Bhonsla, who in October, 1813, combined their forces and laid siege to the town with nearly 70,000 men. The intrepidity of the Nawáb, Wazír Muhammad, beat off this formidable attack, but the danger did not pass away till the end of 1814, and in his distress he applied to the Indian Government for assistance, through Mr. Metcalfe, the Resident at Delhi. Protection was offered to him, October, 1814, on the usual conditions of a subsidiary alliance, and at first the negotiations appeared to offer some prospect of success. On the other hand, Sindhia displayed much displeasure at a proposal which withdrew a victim from his grasp; nor was his disappointment lessened by the fact that on the fall of Bhopál he hoped to reap all the fruits of the victory and, obtaining a lever against his ally the Bhonsla, to gain a preponderating influence over the Maráthá states. The Peshwá and the Rájá of Nágpur also secretly resented the interference in a native state they had been accustomed to harry; and hence, in the winter of 1814–15, when the English were involved in reverses in Nepál, the mutual jealousies of the discordant elements in Central India subsided, and had the Maráthás, Pindárís, and Patháns been ready to strike then, they might have compromised British prestige. But they were not ready, and were overawed by the vigour of the Governor-General, who raised fresh battalions, reinforced Bundelkhand, and concentrated large bodies of troops near the seat of probable disturbance.

Meanwhile Wazír Muhammad had derived no small benefit from these arrangements; he was considered to be under the protection of Calcutta, and interference on his behalf was sufficient to guarantee him from further molestation; but the danger being past, he cooled down in his desire to establish definite relations with the Supreme Government, and the latter, perceiving that events in Central India now took a less acute form, while British arms were again in the ascendent in Nepál, countermanded the military arrangements which had been made and dropped the negotiations with Bhopál.

The scene now changes to Poona, where Bájí Ráo reigned, who was reputed to be a crafty intriguer of unscrupulous character but without much personal bravery. The treaty of Bassein had placed him in a position of dependence, but it also lent him the aid of British bayonets in supporting his rights against his feudatories, and thus he had the means of enforcing claims which otherwise he was powerless to assert. He had rights over other states, notably those of a financial nature over the Gáekwár of Baroda, the origin of which need not be explained here. The Supreme Government, anxious to adjust them on an equitable basis, suggested that the latter's minister, Gangadhar Shástrí,—a firm upholder of British influence,—should go to Poona for this purpose; and this he did in June, 1814, having first obtained a guarantee from Calcutta for his personal safety. The Peshwá, intent on forming a strong anti-British combination among the Maráthá states, hoped to be able to secure the adherence of the Gáekwár to his schemes, by means of this envoy. He therefore concurred in the negotiations proposed, but he failed in his object of gaining the Shástrí to his cause. He was at this time in the hands of a favourite called Trimbakjí, a low-caste Hindu of a very disreputable character who enjoyed his entire confidence, and who had risen by base means to the highest position at Bájí Ráo's court. Aided by this man, the Peshwá succeeded not only in delaying and thwarting the Shástrí's efforts, but also in fomenting intrigues at Baroda, detrimental to the negotiations and to British treaty rights in both those Maráthá states. Mr. Elphinstone, the Resident at Poona, now intervened and protested warmly against these delays, with the result that the Peshwá completely altered his tone, and seemed as anxious to promote the Shástrí's suit as he had formerly endeavoured to ignore it. But the change in his demeanour, although it flattered the envoy, did not alter the loyalty of the latter towards British interests, and Bájí Ráo, urged by Trimbakjí, determined to get rid of him. Having adroitly persuaded Gangadhar to accept a proposal, against his better judgment, which was rejected at Baroda, the Peshwá and his favourite conceived a violent animosity against him, which, carefully concealed, was soon to end in a serious catastrophe. In July, 1815, the Shástrí was inveigled into accompanying them to a distant Hindu shrine, and was there treacherously and barbarously murdered.

Trimbakjí's guilt was clear, and that of the Peshwá scarcely admitted of any doubt, but the latter vehemently protested his own innocence, and his personal repudiation of the crime was accepted; the victim, however, was an accredited envoy, whose safety was specially guaranteed by the Governor-General, and the murder had to be avenged. The Resident therefore put the Peshwá's sincerity to the test, and immediately demanded the apprehension of the guilty favourite. A crisis now arose; Bájí Ráo hesitated between the sacrifice of a powerful and useful accomplice, and a rupture with the British Government, and thus every subterfuge was exhausted, and delay resorted to to save the culprit; but Mr. Elphinstone remained firm to his reasonable demand, and at last, on the 11th of September, Trimbakjí was surrendered and confined in a fort near Bombay. This incident being terminated, the negotiations which had been interrupted were renewed, but the Peshwá took little interest in them, devoting himself with more zest to the formation of a Maráthá combination against British supremacy. On the other hand, the murder of a high-caste Bráhman which had been committed almost before the eyes of the foremost Maráthá prince lowered his cause in public estimation, while the manner in which the crime had been avenged by the Resident gave Government an advantage when the struggle became imminent.

As former representations, sent to England, referring to the atrocities perpetrated by the Pindárís, produced no effect, Lord Hastings formulated a more urgent demand on that important matter, in December 1815. He had fully made up his own mind to the necessity of eradicating this evil, and he determined to relieve India of a scourge which was a reproach to government, and which rendered all peaceable development impossible. He proposed, not for the first time, to establish a general confederation of native states under the guarantee of British protection, as the only means of putting down the predatory system, which was daily taking deeper root in the country, and disintegrating the territory under the Company's jurisdiction; he boldly stated that 'if there was no choice left, he should prefer an immediate war with the Maráthás, for which he was fully prepared, to an expensive system of defence against a consuming predatory warfare, carried on clandestinely by the Maráthá powers, wasting our resources, till they might see a practical opportunity of coming to an open rupture.' But his efforts to insure the safety of the Company's possessions were thwarted by his Council at Calcutta, and the plan which he elaborated had therefore to be submitted to England without the concurrence of his colleagues [1].

The home authorities also were still fully persuaded of the wisdom of the policy which had been adopted in 1805, and desired that it should be continued. They were influenced by the fear they entertained for

[1] J. C. Marshman's *Hist. of India*, 3 vols., London, 1867, ii. 312. (Hereafter quoted as *Marshman*.)

the Maráthá princes, more especially for Sindhia; they accordingly urged that peace should be maintained, at any price however degrading, and they enjoined that economy should be practised. Animated by such sentiments they prohibited the Indian Government 'from engaging in plans of general confederacy, and offensive operations against the Pindárís, either with a view to their utter extirpation, or in anticipation of expected danger[1].'

This dispatch was received at Calcutta in April, 1816, but before that date the Pindárís became bolder, as they observed British indifference to their proceedings, and, urged by the Maráthá chiefs, who for their own purposes encouraged them to make their raids in the Company's territories, they subjected the latter to fearful outrages. Towards the close of 1815 they laid waste the Nizám's dominions, penetrating even beyond the Kistná river into the Madras Presidency, and notwithstanding the strenuous exertions made to overtake them, they escaped capture and brought an immense amount of booty back to their haunts in the valley of the Narbadá. Nor was this all, for in the following February they made a still more destructive incursion into the Northern Circars, and devastated a province where security had been enjoyed by fifty years of British rule.

'I have read a letter,' writes the Governor-General, 'from the Guntúr Circar, on the coast, stating a very affecting circumstance. A village was surrounded by the Pindárís.

[1] Marshman, ii. 305.

The horrors perpetrated by these demons at other places made the poor villagers, totally unarmed and incapable of resistance, fly to the desperate resolution of burning themselves with their wives and children. The houses were all of wood and palm-leaf mats; so that most of them being set fire to at once, the dreadful sacrifice was immediately fulfilled. Some boys who had not the courage to bear the flames, escaped, and explained the circumstance. All the remainder of the inhabitants perished; and I am strictly forbidden by the Court of Directors to undertake the suppression of the fiends who occasioned this heart-rending scene, lest I should provoke a war with the Maráthás. Hundreds of women belonging to other villages have drowned themselves in the wells, not being able to survive the pollution they had suffered. All the young girls are carried off by the Pindárís, tied three or four, like calves on a horse, to be sold. . . They carried off booty to the value of more than a million sterling[1].'

In March, 1816, Wazir Muhammad of Bhopál died, and was succeeded by his son Nasír Muhammad, a young prince whose power to sustain his position amid the troubles that surrounded him appeared to be very doubtful: an application was immediately made for protection, but Lord Hastings, being hampered in this matter by the home authorities, had reluctantly to forego the great advantages which he saw must result from a treaty with that state, and was obliged to limit his answer to general sentiments of goodwill and amity.

In the same month, however, an important event took place in Nágpur; Rájá Raghují the reigning

[1] Private Journal, ii. 112.

Bhonsla died, and his son Pursají, being blind and imbecile, was incapable of ruling. Thereupon two chiefs contested the right of being named regent or virtual master of this important principality. Mahdují, Raghují's nephew, commonly called Apá Sáhib, being next heir according to native custom, had the best title to the office, and he enforced his claim by the capture of his rival; but feeling himself still insecure, he proposed the conclusion of a subsidiary alliance with the British Government. The importance of this overture could be scarcely overrated, and it became all the more apparent, even to the Indian Council, after the Pindárí irruption, just mentioned, had shown the apparent ease with which these detestable freebooters were able to devastate with impunity a British province. The Governor-General therefore experienced little difficulty in complying with Apá Sáhib's request, and a subsidiary treaty was signed on the 27th May. By such an alliance, security was obtained for 300 miles of frontier, which up to that time was almost totally unguarded; the secret plans of the Peshwá and of Sindhia to re-establish the Maráthá confederacy, were disconcerted; and a military position was occupied near the Narbadá, from which the territories of the latter prince were exposed to attack, and whence Pindárí raids might in future be more easily intercepted.

'I regard this event as giving me the fairest ground of confidence that I shall be able to achieve all I wish to effect for the Company's interest without any war. This rests on our presumption of the Peshwá's fidelity. If he be treacherous (and there is no answering for a Maráthá), we might have a struggle; but the consequences of such a contest could not now be doubtful, and it would only make the ultimate arrangement more beneficial to the Company[1].'

True to his policy of endeavouring to rid the country of the disorders occasioned by predatory bands of armed freebooters, Lord Hastings had meanwhile turned his attention to Rájputána. In March, 1816, Jagat Singh, Rájá of Jaipur, being almost overpowered by Amír Khán, urgently prayed for British protection; the Governor-General had been empowered to comply with such a request, by authority dated December, 1813, and, after some difficulty, succeeded in persuading his Council that it was proper to offer him a subsidiary alliance. Jagat Singh, however, delayed the negotiations which followed, so that it was not till later that the treaty was definitely concluded; but he gained the advantage which the concentration of 40,000 British troops near Rájputána afforded, and this display of force, made for the purpose of defending the proposed arrangements, convinced Amír Khán that the Supreme Government was at length determined to put a stop to the anarchy which he was causing in that distracted district.

In the season 1816–17, the Pindárís pursued again the same tactics as in the previous year. They invaded British territory, 23,000 strong, and ravaged many parts of the country, from Ahmadnagar in the

[1] Private Journal, ii. 125.

west of the Indian continent to the Northern Circars in the east, and attempted even to devastate the province of Cuttack. Divided into numerous bands, and moving simultaneously to different places far apart from each other, they traversed a much larger extent of territory than they had ever done before, and caused a wide-spread terror by their ferocious and merciless excesses. At first they succeeded in eluding the vigilance of the troops sent in their pursuit; but extraordinary precautions had been taken, and an army large enough to engage in an important campaign had been collected; and thus in the course of the winter, many of the Pindárí bands were fortunately overtaken, attacked, and destroyed.

Lord Hastings was by no means satisfied with these partial successes, and waited with impatience for authority to root out altogether this lawless association. He had been thwarted in his endeavour to do so by the opinions of his colleagues, and by instructions received from England. These, being conceived in a spirit of exaggerated dread of the Maráthá power, produced a passive policy of defence, which was wholly ineffectual against incursions of predatory hordes, whose irruptions extended over a wide range of frontier. He clearly saw that the tranquillity, and even the safety, of British possessions demanded the destruction of that dangerous race of banditti. He had no sympathy whatsoever with the vacillation displayed at home, nor with the timorous policy it dictated, and he repudiated with scorn a suggestion that the Pindárís might be overcome by intrigue, by setting chief against chief, and by fomenting internal disputes among them. 'When the Honourable Committee,' he said, 'suggest the expediency of engaging one portion of the Pindárí association to destroy another, I am roused by the fear that we have been culpably deficient in pointing out to the authorities at home the brutal and atrocious qualities of these wretches ... and I am confident that nothing would have been more repugnant to the feelings of the Honourable Committee, than the notion that the Government should be soiled by a procedure, which was to bear the colour of a confidential intercourse in a common cause with any of these gangs[1].' He knew that the evil must be crushed, without the concession of any terms to anarchy, and he was convinced that it could be suppressed if the determination to do so existed; he believed moreover that the native princes would have to submit to its removal, without attempting seriously to interfere with the adoption of such a course.

Meanwhile the Board of Control in England, enlightened by the events of 1815–16, which could no longer be explained away, had tardily, in September, 1816, addressed a letter to the Governor-General, giving him a reluctant and qualified authority to suppress the Pindárís, and to destroy their future means of action. But before this letter had reached Calcutta, his advisers in the Indian Council were frightened at the ravages which had been perpetrated

[1] Marshman, ii. 317.

in British territory in the season 1816–17, and they at last agreed that 'the resolution adopted of refraining from any system of offensive operations against the Pindárís, till the sanction of the Court could be received, should be abandoned, and that vigorous measures for the suppression of the Pindárís had become an indispensable object of public duty[1].' Armed with this important decision, without which he was powerless to act, Lord Hastings now took his own measures; and having made up his mind definitely on the plan to be pursued, and upon its feasibility, he determined on the 21st December to attack the Pindárís, and he gave immediate notice of this intention, to be carried out in spite of obstacles which might be raised by open or secret foes[2].

The execution of this project was necessarily delayed until the following autumn, 1817; but in the meanwhile the Supreme Government was not inactive, and in addition to the military arrangements necessary for the undertaking, prepared for the contingencies that were likely to arise. It was evident to the Governor-General that the annihilation of the predatory system must entail a thorough change in the conditions then existing in Central India. The evil that grew there in such alarming proportions was no accidental circumstance; in his opinion it was the

[1] Marshman, ii. 320; P. Auber's *Rise and Progress of the British Power in India*, 2 vols., London, 1837 (hereafter quoted as *Auber*), ii. 519; Private Journal, ii. 153.

[2] Prinsep, i. 411.

direct result of chronic anarchy, which arose from the inordinate and unchecked ambition indulged in by the native rulers. All these princes were scrambling for personal power, and not one of them was safe from the inroads of his neighbours; their councils were divided, and their tributaries in constant rebellion; their armies were continually clamouring for their pay, and their military leaders in a perpetual state of insubordination; they observed no duties, and they acknowledged no rights; society under their guidance was crumbling into ruins, and their subjects were pursuing their own selfish advantages. It was only natural, then, that men should combine to plunder and to devastate, and should continue to do so until there was a complete revolution in the native ideas of government. Without a reform in the lands subject to Maráthá influence, the reign of rapine must flourish, and if put down by force it must revive again like a noxious weed, and occasion ever-recurring exertions to give some temporary immunity from its ravages.

The conclusion was obvious, and the remedy could only be found in the imperial system introduced by Lord Wellesley. Some great power must arise in India, and weld the whole mass into a solid and civilised confederacy, bound together by the supremacy of public law and respect for international obligations, where the weak would find protection, and where all could enjoy security for their legitimate rights. India had been accustomed to a lord paramount, whom all acknowledged, and who in a fashion settled disputes, and checked the ambition of the strong; the absence of such a power, however imperfectly wielded by the Mughals, had produced disorder, and had interfered with the prosperity of British possessions. England alone could occupy this position, and the assumption of so onerous a responsibility was not only the natural result of her commanding prestige and ascendency in the East, but was also the direct consequence of the Governor-General's determination to stamp out altogether the bands of organised freebooters that infested the country.

Lord Hastings did not despair of carrying out his design by peaceable means, and spared no pains to induce the native chiefs to co-operate with him against the Pindárís; he hoped to establish in this manner a community of interests, by which to arrive at an understanding with the most considerable princes of Central India, and so promote the public and general tranquillity. In his own words, 'it was his boast to have an earnest desire to accomplish everything by pacific means, and to be able to declare with sincerity, that the exclusive object of his present preparations was to get rid of the greatest pest that society ever experienced'; and if he had not the full sanction of the home authorities upon the measures he proposed, yet he took the whole responsibility of this action upon himself, and felt sure that the result would justify him in the eyes of British public opinion[1]. But he did not disguise from himself that negotiations might

[1] Prinsep, ii. 23.

fail. He was aware that he had not merely to disperse a band of brigands, but to destroy a system which had taken deep root in the native states. Interference with this system must entail hostility from powerful Maráthá chiefs, who, busily engaged in plotting against the British authority, and accustomed to the licence of unbounded independence, were scarcely to be restrained by treaties, however solemn and binding. The attitude of the native states gave cause for much anxiety, and a war once begun against the Pindárís might easily extend, and produce a general conflagration. Hence arrangements, both political and military, had to be made to meet many contingencies. The nature of these arrangements will be described in the next chapter; but before closing the present one it will be necessary to recapitulate briefly the dispositions of the native princes most concerned in the coming struggle, at the important juncture (end of 1816) when the determination was formed to crush the Pindárís.

The Peshwá was outwardly on good terms with the Supreme Government, but he had been humiliated by events succeeding the Shástrí's murder, and his underhand energy had not diminished, nor did he cease his secret schemes of revenge and ambition, which he continued to push on with unremitting vigour. Apá Sáhib, regent of Nágpur, was apparently content with British protection, and was interested for the present in preserving good relations with Calcutta; but he was a new and untried ruler, and his professions of loyalty could not be much relied upon. It has already been mentioned that the court of the young Holkar, Malhár Ráo, was in confusion, owing to the contests going on between his father's widow, Tulsí Bái, and Amír Khán (who acted through his relation and agent, Gafur Khán); these two parties came to an open rupture in the winter of 1816–1817, but neither side gained any very great advantage over the other. Owing to these complications, the British Government had had very few communications with Holkar since 1808. Dáulat Ráo Sindhia was one of the most powerful of the Maráthá princes, and his hostility was specially to be feared; after having been foiled in his schemes against Bhopál and the Bhonsla Rájá by the action of Lord Hastings, he endeavoured to assist the Peshwá in his plan of consolidating Maráthá influences, and he favoured the Pindárís by promising to support them and by directly inciting them to ravage the Company's territory; but his power was temporarily reduced by internal dissensions and by disorganization among his troops. It was well understood that both Sindhia and Holkar were too much interested in maintaining the predatory system not to support it to the utmost extent of their means, should their internal difficulties be arranged and their circumstances enable them to take the offensive. No anxiety was felt for the attitude of the Gáekwár's government, and it was hoped that Bhopál and many of the Rájput chiefs would be favourably disposed to British plans; but there was some uneasiness with regard to the Nizám, for his subjects were restless and excitable, and had only recently been roused by a rising—happily unsuccessful—which had been attempted by the sons of that prince.

It was clear then that a crisis of no small magnitude was impending,—one which was likely to produce an important effect upon the fortunes of the Company in India, and to form one of the principal landmarks in the history of the progress of British power in Asia.

CHAPTER VI

THE STRUGGLE, 1817. THE PINDÁRÍ WAR. THE MARÁTHÁ POWERS RISE IN REVOLT.

IN order to carry out the great policy of reform which he contemplated in India, the Governor-General first proceeded by negotiation to enlist the co-operation of the native princes against the Pindárís and to prevent a combination in their favour; he neglected no ruler that could be useful to his design, and assumed the principle that in the coming struggle none could be neutral. He endeavoured therefore to improve relations with Poona and Nágpur, and approached Sindhia, Holkar, many chiefs in Central India and in Rájputána, and even Amír Khán, whom he hoped to conciliate and wean from his irregular and disorderly conduct. Subsidiary treaties were accordingly, in 1817, concluded with several states in the province of Málwá, and with Nasír Muhammad of Bhopál, who proved himself to be a staunch and faithful ally; in Rájputána also, the negotiations with Jagat Singh of Jaipur, which had been delayed, induced the Rájás of Udaipur and of Jodhpur and others to apply for protection, and towards the end of the year alliances were formed with them, enabling the Supreme Government to deal with disorder in Western Hindustán in a more effectual manner than otherwise would have been the case.

Meanwhile affairs had not prospered at Poona. In September, 1816, Trimbakjí—the Shástrí's murderer and the Peshwá's evil genius—after scarcely a year's imprisonment, escaped, and, eluding every effort made for his recapture, disappeared from sight for a few months. Bájí Ráo disowned his favourite to the Resident, and even assumed a conciliatory attitude, professing himself in hearty sympathy with the project against the Pindárís, and concluding a reasonable accommodation with the Gáekwár, February, 1817. But all this time he was covertly in league with Trimbakjí himself, and together they were actively preparing a formidable insurrection against British influence and treaty rights in this Maráthá state. The treachery having been discovered, fortunately before it came to a head, Mr. Elphinstone declared his intention of sending the subsidiary force to disperse the levies which were being illegally made, and if necessary to coerce the Peshwá to refrain from further aggression. The latter endeavoured to gain time, but the Resident, long accustomed to his tortuous policy and persistent hostility, brooked no further delay, reinforced the British contingent by that of Haidarábád, ordered a strong detachment to Poona, and presented that perfidious prince with an ultimatum. Bájí Ráo, now thoroughly alarmed, yielded to a demand to surrender three forts as a guarantee for the future, but he still refused to discountenance the proceedings of the Trimbakjí.

A disturbance at Cuttack having at this crisis occasioned a delay in the transmission of the Governor-General's instructions upon the circumstances which had arisen, Elphinstone acted on his own responsibility, and on the 6th May gave the Peshwá a month of grace within which to cease all connection with his favourite. A few days later the instructions so anxiously expected reached Poona, and therein three contingencies were considered and provided for:—If Bájí Ráo consented to deliver up Trimbakjí, and honestly endeavoured to put a stop to the disturbance which he caused, before the arrival of the instructions, then the treaty of Bassein, although grossly violated by recent events, was to be renewed in its old form; if, after this date, he fulfilled his obligations, the treaty was to be modified, and additional security taken against an untrustworthy ally; and lastly, if he refused, and still persisted in his hostility, he was to be deposed. The month was slipping by; the Resident took possession of the three forts, collected his forces, and was preparing for action, when the Peshwá, finding all further resistance useless, at last issued a proclamation offering a substantial reward for the apprehension of the escaped murderer, and thereby enabled Elphinstone to come to terms with him by a fresh compact, which, signed the 13th June, replaced the relations established at Bassein in 1802.

By the treaty of Poona, Trimbakjí was outlawed and his family handed over as hostages, the subsidiary force in Bájí Ráo's dominions was increased, and the treaty of Bassein was renewed subject to certain modifications; of these the most important were, that the Peshwá renounced all intrigues in Central India and the suzerainty of the Maráthá confederacy; he ceded the sea-board province of Konkan, parts of the Deccan, several of his strongholds, and his rights over Málwá, in Bundelkhand, and elsewhere in Hindustán north of the Narbadá. Before the signature of this new arrangement the insurrection had been put down by force, and shortly after the events just recorded, Trimbakjí was driven into the Vindhya mountains.

Bájí Ráo had displayed little wisdom in these transactions, and derived no benefit therefrom. Profuse in insincere professions, and systematically violating his solemn engagements, he had not the patience to wait till his plans were ripe, nor the fortitude to bear the responsibility which an open revolt entailed. His pusillanimous duplicity was without any excuse, and on the eve of the Pindárí war, it might in justice have been severely punished; but he was leniently dealt with nevertheless, and only sufficient security was taken against him to ensure his good behaviour in the future. Yet he learnt nothing by experience, for he continued to plot against British power, and in October, under pretence of preparing to assist in the suppression of brigandage, he was collecting a force with which he vainly imagined he could reassert his former independence and rid himself of the control he hated.

Nor was this the only prince bound by a subsidiary treaty who caused anxiety at this moment. On the 1st February Pursají Bhonsla was found murdered in his palace, and a successor had to be appointed; the conduct of Apá Sáhib, the regent, was not free from suspicion with respect to the crime, yet there was no evidence to prove his participation in it, and, as he was the next heir, he was recognised as the new Bhonsla. Finding himself now firmly fixed upon the *Masnad* as ruler of Nágpur, and no longer requiring British support to assert his position, he soon altered his demeanour, and joined the Maráthá intrigues that were going on against the Government of Calcutta. The collapse of the Peshwá's aspirations, it is true, effected a change, and he resumed his former conciliatory attitude; but only for a time, for in the autumn he was again known to be conspiring against British rights, and when the war began in November, arrangements had almost immediately to be made to counteract the hostility which he displayed, and which at last proved fatal to his dynasty.

If affairs gave anxiety in the south, they were not more satisfactory in the north. The geographical importance of Daulat Ráo's territories in the approaching contest, and the power which that prince had to thwart or to facilitate the military operations that were in contemplation, had early engaged the serious attention of the Supreme Government. Application having been made to Sindhia, in September, for authority to march troops across his territories from the Deccan into the valley of the Narbadá, the Maharájá, pressed by his soldiery and relying upon the Peshwá, evaded the demand; he certainly pretended to be intent on the destruction of the Pindárís, and affected anxiety to co-operate by undertaking an expedition against them on his own account. But the Governor-General was in no humour to be thwarted by dissimulation, and, having full knowledge of his aggressive intentions, sent him a formal note of solemn remonstrance. This communication, containing a long catalogue of grievances, declared that they amounted to a dissolution of existing treaties under which alone Sindhia's independence was secured; it further demanded his cordial and unqualified support in the Pindárí war, and warned him that his failure to comply with the requisition would be regarded as an act of hostility. There was abundant proof to substantiate the assertions which had been made, and it was vigorously used to disarm this important native state in the coming struggle.

The court of Gwalior, unable to resist this pressure openly, was now obliged to consider the following conditions of an alliance which were offered. The article of the treaty of 1805, by which the Indian Government was debarred from having any relations with the principal chiefs in Málwá and in Rájputána, was to be abrogated; a contingent of 5000 horse was to be placed at the disposal of the Governor-General, to be paid regularly out of funds handed over for that purpose by Daulat Ráo; British military commissioners were to be received at the head-quarters of all his troops, and as a security for good faith, two strongholds were to be retained, viz., Handiá, situated on the Narbadá a little below Hoshangábád, and commanding one of the important passages across the river, and Asírgarh, a stronger fort in the Sátpura mountains. Discussions were continued for a month on this basis, and the usual subterfuges resorted to to gain time and to avoid a definite settlement; the temporary cession of Asírgarh was strenuously resisted, and no conclusion was reached when hostilities broke out.

Negotiations were conducted at the same time with Amír Khán, who was offered a principality about Tonk, formed of the territories he had already acquired from Holkar, on condition that he would disband his army and sell his artillery for five lakhs of rupees to the British Government. Holkar was also approached, and terms proposed similar to those offered to Sindhia, with the addition, however, that the independence of Amír Khán was to be recognised; no answer was received from the court of Indore for some time. The fate of these proceedings and their results will be described presently; meanwhile, such being the general relations existing between the Supreme Government and the principal native chiefs at the end of October, when operations in the field were about to commence, it is necessary to turn to the military preparations which were made simultaneously with the political arrangements just described.

It had been calculated that the following troops could be furnished by the native states, their allies and dependencies, against the British Government when engaged in restoring order in Central India:—

	Horse.	Foot.	Guns.
Sindhia	14,000	16,000	140
Holkar	20,000	8,000	107
Peshwá	28,000	14,000	37
Bhonsla	16,000	18,000	85
Amír Khán	12,000	10,000	200
Pindárís	15,000	1,500	20
Nizám	25,000	20,000	—
Total	130,000	87,500	589[1]

In deciding to crush organised brigandage and all who aided and abetted it, Lord Hastings determined to provide himself with ample means for the purpose. For a long time he had been preparing for the struggle, maturing his plans, and accumulating his resources, and all through the summer of 1817 he was occupied in finally completing his arrangements. The Pindárís were to be rooted out of their haunts which lay in Málwá, somewhat to the east of Ujjain, north of the Narbadá and between Bhopál and the dominions of Sindhia and Holkar; to accomplish this it had been decided to surround them on all sides,—on the north and east from Bengal, on the south from the Deccan,

[1] Colonel V. Blacker's *Memoir of the operations of the British Army in India during the Maráthá War of 1817–19*, London, 1821, p. 19. (Hereafter quoted as *Blacker*.)

and on the west from Gujarát,—and to keep the native states in check. An extended movement, therefore, was about to be made inwards, from the circumference of a great circle, whose centre was somewhere near Handiá and whose diameter was nearly 700 miles in length; the enormous distances which separated the different bases of operations, the absence of rapid means of inter-communication, and the necessity of simultaneous action, all contributed to render the task which had been undertaken an exceedingly difficult one.

Lord Hastings commanded the whole grand army destined to perform this vast concentric operation. It was divided into two armies, the Northern or the Army of Hindustán, and the Southern or that of the Deccan. The latter was placed under Sir Thomas Hislop, to whom was given all military and political authority in the south, subject of course to general directions from the Governor-General; Sir John Malcolm, who also commanded a division, was appointed Political Officer in the Deccan under Hislop.

The Northern Army, led by Lord Hastings in person (29,000 infantry, 14,000 cavalry, and 140 guns), was composed of four divisions and two corps of observation, posted at Mirzápur and on the frontiers of South Behar against an irruption into Bengal. The Central or 1st Division (General Brown) was formed on the Jumna between Kálpi and Etáwah, and was to advance southwards towards Gwalior; the Right or 2nd Division (General Donkin) at Agra, to overawe Sindhia and Amír Khán; the Left or 3rd Division (General Marshall) at Kálinjar in Bundelkhand, to co-operate with the Southern Army on the Narbadá, and, supported by the two corps just mentioned, to communicate with Nágpur and to close the eastern exit of escape to the enemy; and the Reserve Division (Sir David Ochterlony) was concentrated somewhat later at Rewári, to cover Delhi and to act in Rájputána.

Owing to recent events in the Deccan a large number of troops had been employed there, and these when reinforced were formed into the Southern Army, which, organised into six divisions and having the Gujarát corps (under Sir William Keir) attached to it, amounted to 52,000 infantry, 18,000 cavalry, and 160 guns. The 1st and 3rd Divisions of the Army of the Deccan (under Sir T. Hislop and Sir J. Malcolm respectively) were to march from Jálna and Amráoti upon Handiá; the 2nd Division (General Doveton) was ordered to take up a position on the Pengangá in support, and to cover the Nizám's dominions; the 4th Division (General Smith) was placed in the province of Khándesh on the Upper Godávari river, prolonging Doveton's line to the west and communicating with Gujarát; the 5th Division (Colonel Adams) was at Hoshangábád on the Narbadá; the troops engaged in enforcing the stipulations of the treaty of Poona in the south of the Peshwá's dominions were formed (16th November) into the Reserve Division under General Pritzler.

The forces concentrated in 1817, amounting to nearly 120,000 men and 300 guns,—the largest army collected up to that time for one purpose under the British flag in India,—included some 29,000 irregulars and contingents furnished by native princes, and of these 19,000 horse were under English officers; there were also 13,000 European troops distributed evenly among the different divisions, and of these 8,500 were infantry, more than 2,000 cavalry, and the remainder artillery [1].

Lord Hastings reached Cawnpur in September and intended to have at least two divisions on the Narbadá early in October, in order to fall upon the Pindárís when their power of rapid movement was hampered by swollen rivers. But although there had been a drought in the north, the rains were more than usually severe in the Deccan and the concentration of that army had in consequence been delayed; Sir T. Hislop arrived at his head-quarters at Haidarábád in August, and, leaving early in October, did not reach the position close to Handiá he meant to occupy, till the 10th November.

On account of these delays, the Northern Army moved a little later than was at first intended. Lord Hastings attached himself to the Central Division, crossed the Jumna 28th October, and advanced to Siunda on the Sind river. The Right Division left Agra about the same time and marched to Dholpur on the Chambal, and thus early in November two strong corps were posted on the northern frontiers of Sindhia's territories, about sixty miles apart, and

[1] Blacker, p. 25.

scarcely two marches distant from Gwalior. Daulat Ráo was completely surprised by this skilful and unexpected manœuvre; he had barely 8,000 men with him at his capital, the rest of his troops were distributed elsewhere, and he suddenly found himself surrounded and cut off from the other portions of his dominions by two British divisions, who, having seized the passes over the rocky hills between the Chambal and the Sind rivers, blocked his communications to the south. All his hopes of evading the demands which were pressed upon him now disappeared, and he perceived with consternation that while he attempted to engage the Governor-General with unprofitable discussions, the latter had secretly and swiftly swept down upon him, when he was unprepared, and left him no option but to agree at once to the terms which were offered. Sindhia reluctantly concluded the treaty of Gwalior (5th November), the stipulations of which have already been mentioned, but he took care to obstruct its execution by every means in his power; this result was only what was to be expected, and the direct and full effect of the treaty was not immediately felt: that is to say, a decided advantage was gained, and Sindhia who could best support the Pindárís was controlled and neutralised, and was moreover discredited in the eyes of the other Maráthá chiefs; but force alone held him to his contract [1].

Lord Hastings was much elated by the ratification

[1] The text of the Treaty of Gwalior is given in Thornton's *History of the British Empire in India*, 2nd ed., London, 1859, p. 431.

of this important treaty, and expresses himself thus in his Private Journal:—

'Sindhia subscribes to all the conditions which I dictated, and has swallowed a bitter drench in so doing. I should have thought myself oppressive had he not been so thoroughly false a fellow. The engaging to co-operate in the extirpation of the Pindárís, whom he has fostered—to whom he has plighted protection, and who really have hitherto constituted a material part of his strength,—must be deeply mortifying.'

After explaining the main features of the treaty, he goes on:—

'Important as those points are, they fall short in that respect of our emancipation from the article in our treaty of 1805, by which the British Government had debarred itself of the right of entering into relations with any state over which the Maráthás claimed prerogatives. As the Maráthás advanced this pretension with regard to every state of Central India, except Jaipur—this strange gratuitous engagement prevented our forming any confederacy which should check Maráthá combinations. Every state, quite to the Indus, has solicited me to take it under British protection; but I have, till now, been restricted from meeting the petition. In consequence of the present treaty, I shall immediately fashion this league of the western states, guaranteeing to Sindhia or Holkar any acknowledged dues from those states which prescription has established . . . We are in a fair way of achieving arrangements which will afford quiet and safety to millions who have long been writhing under the scourge of the predatory powers, as well as under the ferocious cruelty of the Pindárís. I trust that my soul is adequately grateful to the Almighty for allowing me to be the humble instrument of a change beneficial to so many of my fellow-creatures[1].'

The Pindárís under Kárím, Chítu, and Wasil Muhammad, (each 7,000 to 8,000 horsemen), well aware that measures were in progress for their extinction, attempted to combine during the summer, and held a meeting in the middle of September, to concert some plan for their common safety; but their counsels were divided and jealousies existed among them, so that they could come to no arrangement for their mutual defence; moreover, contrary to previous experience, though the native princes were as anxious as ever to give them protection and urged them to resist, they found to their dismay that none of their patrons were bold enough to give an asylum to their families. Considerably depressed, they remained inactive near Bhilsa and to the west of that place, and lived in hopes that the Maráthás would declare war and divert from them the danger with which they were threatened. Wasil Muhammad was the first to cast off the lethargy that weighed them down, and early in November made a raid into Bundelkhand, contriving to evade General Marshall's advance, by moving round his right flank, and even menaced Bánda, when a detachment sent by the Commander-in-Chief from the Central Division forced him to retreat. Meanwhile on the 12th the circle surrounding them

[1] Private Journal, ii. 231. See also Summary of the Administration of the Indian Government (title set forth in full in footnote *ante*, p. 62, and hereafter quoted for brevity as *Summary &c.*), p. 19.

was gradually contracting; Marshall was on the upper Kana river, where he awaited the advance of the Deccan army and opened up communications with Hoshangábád; Donkin had pushed up the left bank of the Chambal towards Kotah, leaving Dholpur guarded; the Central Division watched Gwalior, and the 1st, 3rd, and 5th Divisions of the Deccan Army were preparing to cross the Narbadá. It was hoped that, about the 22nd, all would be ready to make a simultaneous and general attack upon the position occupied by the Pindárís.

But this arrangement was partially interrupted by the Peshwá, who rose to arms, and by the Bhonsla Rájá, who about the same time manifested signs of unmistakeable hostility. To provide for these events a detachment was immediately despatched towards Nágpur on the 12th, but as the revolt in Poona was much more serious, Sir T. Hislop adopted other measures in the emergency which had thus arisen. Convinced that Asírgarh would not submit, even though ceded by Sindhia by the treaty of Gwalior, and that its occupation was important in the present juncture, he determined to support the forces which were directed upon Poona by retiring with the 1st Division to Burhámpur (close to Asírgarh), and ordered up Doveton's battering train to reduce that stronghold. Lord Hastings heard of the revolt in Poona on the 14th, and fearing lest operations in Málwá might be dislocated by the news, urgently directed the commander in the Deccan on no account to suspend his march northwards, but to leave Generals Smith and Pritzler (the 4th and Reserve Deccan Divisions) to deal with the Peshwá. Hislop receiving this order, left Doveton to summon Asírgarh, and, returning to Málwá, re-crossed the Narbadá on the 2nd December, with the intention of marching to Ujjain.

Meanwhile Marshall, Adams, and Malcolm drove the enemy before them, occupying their lands, which were immediately restored to Sindhia or to Bhopál; no resistance was offered, but the troops were unable to entrap or even attack the bands opposed to them, for they were too quick and in every case made a timely and orderly retreat. The three divisions were now in line, and facing the north-west, and a general advance was ordered, Marshall on the right through Sironj, Adams in the centre, and Malcolm on the left, when it was ascertained that Kárím and Wasil Muhammad had joined their forces and were retreating towards Gwalior, while Chítu was moving in a westerly direction to Holkar's territory and towards Jáwad, where Jaswant Ráo Bháo, one of Sindhia's officers, had offered him support and protection.

Upon this, Malcolm turned sharply after Chítu, but this band had disappeared, and he found himself not only in contact with a few mutinous detachments of Sindhia's army but close to Holkar's forces, who about this time joined in the struggle, as will be explained presently. He therefore deemed it wise to delay his advance, and, collecting the scattered columns of his own division, to allow time for the approach of Sir T.

Hislop. The latter was pushing to Ujjain, and the two divisions effected a junction there on the 12th December, the Gujarát corps being meanwhile ordered up to the same place, in order to prevent the Pindárís from retreating southwards through the province of Khándesh, which had been left open by the counter-march of General Smith upon Poona.

Lord Hastings and the Central Division were left (5th November) on the Sind river, holding Sindhia in check, and ready to intercept the flying Pindárís should they move northwards. An unexpected misfortune now occurred. Cholera had been prevalent in Calcutta during the summer of 1817, and having spread along the banks of the Ganges and Jumna, suddenly appeared in a most violent form in the British camp, where raging for ten days, it decimated the ranks and impaired the efficiency of the troops. On the 10th a move was made to Erich on the Braitwa river, and the new camp being healthy, the epidemic was partially arrested, and towards the end of the month the embarrassments occasioned to military operations were fortunately lessened. Daulat Ráo seizing the opportunity, determined to shake off British control, and offering Kárím and Wasil his protection, invited them to join him at Gwalior. The moment was critical; for, added to Sindhia's hostility, there was Holkar's activity, an uncertainty as to Amír Khán's intentions, and some fear that the Gúrkhas might cause trouble. Lord Hastings hearing at this moment of the Peshwá's revolt and of the

Bhonsla's change of attitude, decided that the northern theatre of war was more important than the southern, and had therefore, as we have seen, directed Sir T. Hislop to continue his march into Málwá and not to allow his attention to be diverted from that quarter. The events just recorded in Gwalior caused the immediate return of the Central Division to the Sind river, enfeebled though the troops were by sickness; at the same time a brigade, previously detached to keep up communications with Marshall's Division, was ordered to cross the river and to intercept the Pindárís, while the force near the Chambal was directed to hold the fords at Dholpur.

On the 10th December the Central Division reached the Sind at a point twenty-eight miles from Gwalior and nearer than Sindhia to the passes, already mentioned, which afforded a communication between that capital and the south. This manœuvre, very similar to the one adopted a month before, had precisely the same effect; for it isolated Daulat Ráo, destroyed his freedom of action, and held him to his engagements. But more than this, it effectually intercepted the Pindáris in their flight northwards, who found themselves hemmed in and in doubt which way to turn and effect their escape. In this predicament they turned to the west, in the hope of forcing a passage through the territories of the Rájá of Kotah; but the latter, resisting the invasion, delayed their movements, so that Marshall's division was able to attack and disperse some of their bands. General Donkin also, who had steadily pushed up the left bank of the Chambal, crossed that river, and on the 17th headed the Pindárís, capturing their baggage and Kárím's family. Pressed on every side the two chiefs were nearly taken, but, turning to the south with some 4,000 men, they fled as rapidly as possible, and in spite of the efforts of Adams, who harassed them as they passed, they escaped into Holkar's country, dispirited and exhausted, reduced in numbers, and having lost all their baggage and goods.

Thus by the end of 1817 the Pindárís had been driven out of Málwá and beyond the Chambal, but although they were greatly disorganised and weakened by their misfortunes, yet they did at last succeed in baffling their pursuers and in breaking through the circle that surrounded them. Immediate efforts were made to dislodge them from their new retreat, but before these operations are related, it will be necessary to revert to events that occurred elsewhere in Central India.

The 4th Deccan Division had scarcely marched away from near Poona to take up the position assigned to it in Khándesh, when Bájí Ráo, who was raising troops ostensibly to attack the Pindárís, concentrated as many as 35,000 men near his capital and refused to send them to the seat of war. This circumstance and others made it apparent to the Resident that a crisis was impending, but unwilling to provoke a quarrel he took no public steps to meet the danger he foresaw, until the 1st November, when he moved the British Brigade, left behind at Poona, under Colonel Burr, to a defensive position near Kirkí, some three miles from the town. General Smith was also recalled from the north, but it was known that he could not arrive before the 10th or 12th, though his advanced troops, pushing on as rapidly as possible, were expected on the 6th; on the other hand a European regiment reached Kirkí on the 30th October. The Peshwá determined to strike before the division could return, and sent a messenger on the 5th to Mr. Elphinstone, with demands which could not be complied with; the latter now perceived that his position at Poona was untenable, and immediately after the interview left for Kirkí, attended by his personal escort. He was barely in time, for Bájí Ráo at the head of a body of troops entered the Residency, plundered the buildings, set them on fire, and destroyed a large amount of valuable property. Having accomplished this act of vandalism, the remainder of his troops marched towards Kirkí and determined to storm the British position. But the latter were in no mood to await the assault; for the Resident, knowing that the fidelity of many of the men had been undermined, decided that defensive tactics were useless, and urging Burr to move forward to meet the enemy, the latter responded willingly to this requisition, and gallantly advanced to the attack[1].

A spirited action took place between 2,800 British troops and about 26,000 Maráthás, lasting from four in the afternoon till dark, when the Peshwá's forces

[1] Blacker, p. 69.

making no impression upon their opponents, fell back upon Poona, leaving 500 men on the field; the same evening the British forces returned to Kirkí with a loss of only 86 men, and there they awaited General Smith, who having been delayed by the enemy's cavalry, arrived before Poona on the 13th. Meanwhile the Peshwá not venturing again to attack the gallant little brigade whose valour and discipline had frustrated all his plans, left it unmolested and wreaked his vengeance by committing acts of savage cruelty upon such British officers who ignorant of the revolt came within his grasp [1].

A junction being effected between the 4th Division and the Brigade, the combined forces marched upon Poona, and on the 16th the left wing under Colonel Milnes crossed the river which guarded the town, at the Yellura ford, in the face of the enemy, who, notwithstanding all their efforts, were unable to resist the passage; early next morning the rest of the troops crossed higher up the river, but they found to their immense regret that the Maráthás had abandoned all their posts and had fled to the south. Poona was at once occupied and the pursuit begun, but the Peshwá was too quick, and, beyond capturing a considerable portion of his artillery and ammunition, no further success was achieved. Arrangements had now to be made for the military security of Poona and its neighbourhood, and for a further advance

[1] Blacker, p. 65, &c.; Captain Grant Duff's *History of the Maráthas*, 3 vols., Bombay, 1863, iii. 297, &c.

against the enemy, who, having unfortunately had time to elude the British army, could not be pursued until the 21st.

The Peshwá first retired to the neighbourhood of Sátára, and carried off the representative of Sivají's family, the Rájá of that place, a prince he justly feared at this crisis in his affairs as a dangerous rival to his throne[1]. His resources were slender in the isolated districts bordering upon Mysore, but in Khándesh his adherents were arming, and there he hoped to gain support from the other Maráthá chiefs; hearing, moreover, that Pritzler (Deccan Reserve Division) was advancing from the south, he marched rapidly to Pandharpur, and, doubling round to the north, he succeeded in evading Smith's pursuit, and made for Wattur, on the direct road to Násik, having passed between Poona and Sirúr. At Wattur he was joined by his confederate Trimbakjí. Smith at once turned after him and reached Sirúr on the 22nd December; from that place he gained rapidly upon the fugitive, and not only headed him, but hemmed him close to the hilly country where his cavalry could move with difficulty. Bájí Ráo was now

[1] The Peshwás, though acknowledged suzerains of the Maráthás, were not of the family of Sivají, the founder of their Empire. They were descended from Bálaji Vishwanáth, the minister or *Peshwá* of Sahu grandson of Sivají (who lived early in the eighteenth century), and practically ruler under that feeble prince. The office becoming hereditary, the Peshwás governed at Poona and formed the Maráthá confederacy: while the descendants of Sivají degenerated into insignificant princes at Sátára and Kohápur. Bájí Ráo was the seventh Peshwá. See Hunter's *Indian Empire*, ed. 1882, p. 261 &c.

obliged again to go southwards, and towards the end of the year he was on the direct road to Poona; here we will leave him for the present, and turn to Nágpur, where events similar to those enacted at Poona were taking place.

Apá Sáhib's attitude towards the Supreme Government continually fluctuated, and he followed with almost slavish precision the example set by the ruler of Poona; when the Peshwá became hostile, the Bhonsla was sure to manifest impatience at British control, and when the former was reduced to obedience, he invariably assumed a peaceable demeanour. Apá Sáhib was in short a typical Maráthá prince; he desired to use British power to attain his own ends, but, discontented with the restraints it imposed, he determined to throw off the yoke it laid upon his rule, and, while lacking the necessary personal courage to effect this object, he employed thereto the arts of duplicity in which he excelled. It was therefore to be expected that as soon as the revolt of Bájí Ráo became known, there would be a crisis at Nágpur.

In this instance however, the defeat of the Maráthás at Kirkí, and the occupation of Poona, as well as Sindhia's difficulties, did not seem to produce any change in his hostility, for, on pretence of massing troops against the Pindárís, he also assumed so threatening an attitude that Mr. Jenkins, the Resident, was obliged to post the British force, left near Nágpur, on a position on the Sítabáldí hills, where it could defend the Residency. Hardly was this step taken than the Bhonsla's army fired upon this position with such effect during the night of the 26th–27th November, that severe loss was incurred. A slight intermission in the attack now took place, but early the following morning the position was assailed in earnest by nearly 20,000 men, and defended by a mere handful of some 1,400 troops, who had no means or opportunity to strengthen the heights they held. The Maráthá army contained some 4,000 Arabs who fought with great ardour; they soon carried one of the hills, and, turning their guns upon the main part of the British defences, they endeavoured to take it by storm, while the remainder of the enemy's forces were advancing to their support. The fortunes of the day seemed desperate, and the battle was all but lost, when three troops of Bengal cavalry, under Captain Fitzgerald, were seen to charge upon the Maráthá horse, and, quickly dispersing them in every direction, they captured some guns, and spread terror and confusion among the enemy's ranks: at this moment, too, the British sepoys, elated at the daring exploit, and seizing the opportunity when panic had disorganised the Arabs, charged with new-born enthusiasm, and retook the post which they had previously lost. These successes ended the battle, for the Maráthás, now losing all their former courage, yielded at all points, and were driven back with disgrace; at noon the day was won, and the danger over.

The losses of the contending armies were about the same, but the proportion of those of the enemy could not compare with the numbers who fell on the British side, amounting on that eventful occasion to a fifth of the whole force; yet the Maráthás were dejected and disorganised by their failure, and, refusing to attack again, time was given for fresh troops to arrive and relieve the sorely pressed defenders from the serious embarrassments that surrounded them. Reinforcements soon reached them, from Hoshangábád and elsewhere, and, on the 15th December, the greater part of Doveton's (2nd Deccan) Division, having given up all thoughts of reducing Asírgarh in the present emergency, marched into camp, and enabled Mr. Jenkins to impose his own terms upon the rebellious Rájá. The Bhonsla's personal surrender was effected without delay; but the disbandment of his army and the surrender of his artillery being resisted, it became necessary to enforce both these demands by arms; this was successfully accomplished on the 16th, when the Maráthás were routed and dispersed, and all their guns, stores, and elephants captured. The Arabs however fled into the town, and, holding the citadel, they even repulsed an attempt to take the place by storm, but eventually they voluntarily surrendered on honourable conditions, and were escorted to Khándesh, where they were set free to go where they liked, except to Asírgarh.

These successes were completed by others which were gained elsewhere in the Bhonsla's dominions, where partial revolts had taken place, and the

Resident was now able to regulate more permanent relations with Nágpur. Lord Hastings, on hearing of the events which have been described, decided that Apá Sáhib had forfeited his throne, and ordered his immediate deposition; the sequel of that prince's career proves the wisdom of this decision, but these instructions were delayed, and Mr. Jenkins had meanwhile already offered terms by which the Bhonsla was allowed to retain a nominal sovereignty; he was therefore obliged to adhere provisionally to his proposals, pending further communications from Government, and on the 6th January a draft treaty was signed, approved of subsequently by the Governor-General, by which the Bhonsla ceded Berar and territory near the Narbadá, and consented to rule for the future through ministers to be selected by the Resident; he surrendered all military power, promising to give up his forts should they be demanded, and accepting a British garrison in his own capital.

The course of affairs in the Deccan, in spite of dangers and treachery, had been satisfactory; it was not less so in the north. Amír Khán proved easier to deal with than had been at first imagined, and, as he was one of the principal leaders of the predatory system, the event was of considerable importance. Perceiving how easily Sindhia had been coerced, he allowed his envoy at Delhi to sign, 9th November, a treaty on the conditions which have already been described, and its ratification was expected in a month. Meanwhile the revolt in the Deccan had occurred, and for a time it was uncertain whether he would abide by the treaty or not, more especially since his Sirdars bitterly resented the stipulation which cut them adrift without sufficient compensation. But the successes at Poona and Nágpur, his own inclinations, and his position between General Donkin on the Chambal and Sir D. Ochterlony (who advanced from Rewári to the south of Jaipur), contributed to bring about an amicable settlement, and the treaty was definitely accepted on the 19th of December. Thenceforward Amír Khán proved himself a peaceable ally, and the Pindárís lost his support just when they most required it. Ochterlony remained in the vicinity and, placing himself skilfully between the two principal divisions of the Pathán forces, he effected the disarmament of the greater portion of this army in January and February without the necessity of striking a blow; the artillery was surrendered, and some of the best troops were drafted temporarily into the British service, where they found employment congenial to their restless dispositions. The last body of these mercenary bands was disbanded in March.

It has also been mentioned that Lord Hastings approached Holkar's court. No answer was received till the 15th November, when the regent, Tulsí Bái (widow of the late Holkar), offered to put herself and the young prince under British protection. No one was deceived by those overtures, which seemed to present little chance of leading to any satisfactory result, but General Donkin was nevertheless directed to give effect to the negotiations should they prove successful. The Peshwá's defection however, on becoming known, produced its inevitable result, and Holkar's troops, exhibiting the greatest enthusiasm in Bájí Ráo's cause, and hoping to obtain their arrears of pay through his bounty, began to move southwards to his aid, when they were met by the Pindárí Chítu, closely pursued by Sir J. Malcolm. The movement of the latter upon Ujjain, and his junction with Sir T. Hislop, 12th December, have already been noticed; after which the two British divisions advanced to a point near Mehidpur, where Holkar lay with his army. Attempts to enter into negotiations with him failed; his followers, divided among themselves, and torn by faction, would listen to no accommodation, and, on the 20th December, they combined under the leadership of the Pathán, Gafur Khán, to seize and murder the Bái, whom they suspected of being favourable to a British alliance.

Hostilities were now inevitable, and Hislop, finding peace impossible, determined to attack a troublesome and disorderly army, whose conduct resembled more that of a band of plunderers than the operations of the forces of a responsible state. On the 21st he advanced to Mehidpur, where the enemy were found strongly posted in two lines on the Siprá river. Crossing a ford in front of the position, he assaulted it with his divisions, and, though the enemy's artillery was well served and did considerable execution, their flanks were soon crushed, and the whole army put to irretrievable flight. Their losses amounted to 3,000 men, and their camp, military stores, and seventy guns fell into the hands of the victors, whose casualties however were as much as 800 men. Malcolm was now sent in pursuit, and followed Holkar in a north-westerly direction towards Mandesar.

The Gujarát Division ought to have been present at the battle, but its progress to Ujjain had been delayed by the Bombay government, who feared that the troubles at Poona might extend to Baroda. Lord Hastings however did not share this apprehension, and disapproving of this unnecessary diversion of a strong column at a critical moment, ordered its immediate return to the east, and a junction with Hislop was effected on the 30th. But before Mandesar was reached, Holkar had already, 6th January, accepted a subsidiary treaty, and had consented to give up his claims in Rájputána and elsewhere which had occasioned past disorders; Gafur Khán also, urged thereto by Amír Khán, gave up his career as a leader of mercenaries, and was granted possession of a territorial fief, before it was known that he was concerned in the murder of Tulsí Bái.

Scattered portions of Holkar's army escaped pursuit, and some of them were dispersed in January; the remainder took part later in operations against the British; but the transactions just described settled once for all the disorders which prevailed in the Indore state ever since 1808; the government was reformed and reconstructed on a more solid foundation, and thereafter it ceased to be a menace to public tranquillity.

CHAPTER VII

The final overthrow of the Maráthá Powers

1818–19

The new year opened with bright prospects, for in the short space of the few weeks during which the campaign had lasted, no reverses had been experienced, and many advantages had been gained. The Pindárís, driven from their haunts in the valley of the Narbadá, sought a precarious refuge on the left bank of the Chambal, and were deprived of the assistance of their principal allies; for Holkar was defeated and Amír Khán disarmed; even Sindhia was powerless to help them, and his Sirdars could only afford them a feeble protection in the outlying province of Mewár. In the Deccan also, the formidable insurrections of the Peshwá and of the Bhonsla Rájá had been dealt with promptly; the former lost his capital and was a fugitive in his own dominions, while the latter was reduced to a position of mere nominal sovereignty in Nágpur.

The array of forces employed to achieve these results was imposing beyond all former precedent, but the duties to be fulfilled were proportionately onerous and important, and Lord Hastings, who left nothing to chance, determined to be ready for every contingency that might arise. The Maráthá chiefs had been long endeavouring to take advantage of the weakness displayed in 1805, and their schemes were ripe for execution in 1817; a formidable and—as far as anarchical principles would admit of it—a concerted rising was prepared to accomplish this object. The Supreme Government therefore had many enemies to face, and the events just related show how dangerous it would have been to attempt the destruction of the Pindárís unless large measures of defence had also been adopted, and simultaneous action planned in many distant quarters. The success of the military movements, the timely concentration of large bodies of troops marching from divergent bases, and the subsequent dispositions made to meet the numerous requirements of a complicated campaign, prove the care bestowed on the preliminary arrangements, and exhibit the watchful intelligence of the Commander-in-Chief, who directed every detail of the operations in the field, and guided all the negotiations in the political sphere.

But in spite of the large number of forces deployed, grave risks were also incurred, and twice in the course of a short campaign were small corps, posted at vulnerable points and guarding important interests, exposed to almost certain destruction at the hands of overwhelming masses of the enemy. Disaster had been fortunately avoided by the bravery and discipline of the weak brigades at Poona and Nágpur, and it was due to the efficiency of the English officers who led the natives into action that the battles of Kirkí and the Sítabáldí hills had not been lost. It was impossible to calculate beforehand upon these victories; but the British sepoys, having imbibed habits of military discipline, rallied round their leaders and withstood the onslaught of the enemy, who as a mob were subject to panic and became demoralised by the first reverse. Hence was success achieved under the most unpromising circumstances; and the brilliant result enhanced the prestige of the power of England and the fame of her valour, and carrying dejection among the Maráthá princes, impressed them with the invincible character of the opponents against whom they contended. Yet much remained to be accomplished. The predatory system was not eradicated, and many of its upholders were still in arms; time had been given to Bájí Ráo to escape from the 4th Deccan Division, and he gathered sufficient power to maintain the struggle he began; and, lastly, Apá Sáhib had not been deposed, and latitude enough was conceded to him to continue the conspiracy in which he had embarked.

When the Pindárís were forced into Mewár, General Marshall (Left Division) was ordered back to Sironj, to settle the lands they evacuated, and to prevent their return to their old haunts; Adams marched to Gungrar and Donkin to Sháhpura, to guard the districts in the east and north respectively; a lightly equipped column, composed of troops drawn from the Left and

Central Hindustán Divisions, and placed under the command of General Brown, was also pushed to the south of Kotah, and in communication with Adams; the battle of Mehidpur had moreover rendered the 1st, 3rd, and Gujarát Divisions available to act against the Pindárís from the south. All these forces were to close in as had been done before, and to hunt the freebooters from their new retreat.

As there was now no fear that any considerable force could attack small detachments, the pursuit was carried on by numerous light columns unencumbered by heavy artillery; but the rapidity of the enemy, the difficulties of movement and supply in a rugged and little-known district, the support clandestinely given by native chiefs, and the obstacles thrown in the way of procuring correct information, rendered the service peculiarly arduous and harassing to the troops engaged, and frequently frustrated the plans of the commanders. The operations, however, served in a great measure to pacify the country so traversed, and in this manner Sindhia's officer Jaswant Ráo Bháo who commanded at Jáwad was reduced to order, and punished for harbouring the freebooters. Meanwhile the three Pindárí bands finding no shelter in Mewár, determined to retrace their steps and to return to Málwá by circuitous routes. Chítu was by far the most capable leader, and had lost less than Kárím or Wasil in the first operations; he succeeded in baffling pursuit with the small loss of part only of his baggage, in spite of the strenuous efforts of Sir W. Keir (Gujarát

Division) to capture him, and reached a point near Handiá; but his good fortune soon deserted him, for his approach was discovered, and a detachment from that station came up in time and dispersed his band. Nor were Kárím and Wasil able to escape, for on the 13th they were completely surprised and destroyed by Adams.

Towards the end of January, then, all the organised bodies of Pindárís were annihilated, and judging that it was time to offer the few scattered remnants some inducement to return to a peaceable manner of existence, they were now invited to submit by a message sent them through the Nawáb of Bhopál, and were promised a settlement on lands remotely situated from the scenes of their former depredations. Kárím quickly responded, and obtained lands in Gorakhpur, where he remained with his family and followers, numbering six hundred persons [1]. His example was followed by many others; but Wasil flying to Sindhia remained at large, until that prince was obliged to surrender him, and he was then made a prisoner; he was detained at Gházípur, but some months afterwards on attempting to escape he failed to get away, and committed suicide. Chítu became a wanderer and was deserted by the best part of his band, but he disdained to surrender, and made his way to the Deccan, where he joined the remnants of the Maráthá forces that still maintained themselves in the field. A year later he met with a terrible fate; on being refused admittance into Asírgarh, he went alone into

[1] Wilson, viii. 297.

the jungle much infested by tigers, and disappeared; a few days later his horse was found browsing near the forest, and, on a search being made, his head was discovered and his face recognised, and, near by, some traces of his mangled remains left no doubt that the miserable man had been devoured by a tiger.

Affairs in the northern part of Central India being now nearly settled, new military dispositions were made (2nd February) by Lord Hastings, to suit the altered circumstances of the war. Donkin's force (the Central Division), and the two corps of observation in the East were broken up and marched back to their peace quarters; but troops were still kept between Bundelkhand and Etáwah to hold Sindhia in check until the final settlement should be made in that state. Sir D. Ochterlony was left in Rájputána. Marshall's division was reinforced and ordered to take possession of the territories ceded by Apá Sáhib near the Narbadá; this General, moreover, annexed the principality of Ságar, where the Rájá, on account of his persistent hostility and defiant disregard of treaties, had been condemned by the Governor-General to lose his fief; operations in this quarter lasted until the end of April. The Maráthá princes were by this time isolated, and no further reunion on a formidable scale was possible among them; the moment had therefore arrived when those that still remained in arms could be more easily pacified by the local civil and military authorities, under control and directions from Calcutta; and the necessity for unity of command having ceased in the Deccan, the Southern Army was dissolved.

The divisions under Generals Keir, Doveton, Smith, and Adams were constituted out of the subsidiary forces stationed in Gujarát, Haidarábád, Poona, and Nágpur, respectively, and the intention was to send these troops back to their proper stations as soon as circumstances would permit. To this end, part of the Gujarát corps was marched towards Baroda; but Doveton was ordered to Khándesh; and Adams was retained north of the Narbadá for a short time, and was occupied in receiving the submission of the Pindárís, and in taking possession of the districts that were ceded. The 1st Deccan Division also proceeded to Khándesh, and, on the way, reduced some forts which were held by Holkar's commanders in defiance of the treaty of Mandesar. The 3rd Deccan Division, under Malcolm, was kept in Holkar's dominions north of the Narbadá, in order to pacify that district and introduce a stable form of government there; this force, moreover, reduced the district of Soandwara, lying east of the Chambal and north of Ujjain, where the marauding spirit still survived. Holkar's troops were employed and rendered good service upon this occasion, and the fact afforded satisfactory proof that the system adopted by Lord Hastings in his dealings with the Maráthá chiefs was likely to be successful.

The only point of importance left unprovided for by the dispositions, just described, was the reduction of the fort of Asírgarh, held by one of Sindhia's

Killadars (Commandants); at one time it was proposed to undertake the task at once, but it was deferred. The subjugation of Khándesh, a province full of strongholds, and inhabited by warlike Arab colonies, was a more pressing necessity, since it afforded support to the Peshwá, whose submission was of the utmost importance. It is now time to turn to the operations directed against that prince.

Bájí Ráo, having been foiled in his attempt to penetrate into Khándesh, was left north of Poona apparently in full march upon his capital. Colonel Burr, the commandant, fearing lest this was a deliberate intention to raise a storm in a turbulent city only lately occupied and imperfectly subdued, sent to Sirúr for reinforcements. Thereupon Captain Staunton was ordered to march without delay to Poona at the head of 500 infantry, 250 cavalry, and two guns, and left camp at eight in the evening on the 31st December. Next morning when about half way he unexpectedly found himself intercepted by the whole of the Peshwá's army, numbering 20,000 horse, and 8,000 foot (of whom nearly half were Arabs—troops far more formidable than the ordinary natives). There was no possibility of getting away from these hostile masses, and Staunton, avoiding the plain, had barely time to push to the village of Koregáon to seek a precarious shelter in the danger that threatened him. In this effort he was only partially successful, for the Arabs, perceiving his object, advanced to the village, and occupying some of the best positions it afforded, resisted successfully all attempts to dislodge them.

The little force took up the most favourable line they could find among the buildings they had fortunately seized; but they had been marching all night without food or refreshment, and to add to their embarrassments there was no water to be procured. Cooped up in this miserable position, exhausted by fatigue and want, they engaged in the desperate struggle that now awaited them. The enemy luckily was very weak in artillery, and his cavalry was unable to join in the action, but there was sufficient infantry at hand, and these surged forward in dense masses, wave following wave against the devoted band that resisted their fury. The British officers headed repeated sallies, and gallantly maintained their ground until night-fall, when a gun was captured, and the situation became terribly alarming. The Arabs now thinking they had carried the whole position, began to murder the wounded, and became demoralised; a last counter-attack was then made with such vigour upon the disorganised rabble, that the gun was retaken and the enemy driven back with much slaughter. The crisis past, the Maráthás as usual got discouraged, and after nine hours' fighting they retired out of the village, which Staunton immediately occupied.

The night was passed in the greatest anxiety, and a renewal of the attack was expected; but the Peshwá showed no signs of doing so, and he was seen to move towards the south. Staunton, cut off from

Poona, determined to return to camp, and the better to deceive the enemy, gave out that he meant to continue his march to his original destination; thereupon the Maráthá horse made ready to fall upon him in the plains, but they got no such satisfaction, for when it was dark he retreated quietly to Sirúr, where he arrived on the morning of the 3rd, with his guns and his wounded, 'drums beating and colours flying.'

This brilliant defence added one more exploit to the long roll of British military achievements in India, where want of numbers was compensated by coolness in judgment and bravery in a desperate hour of peril; but it was dearly purchased, for although the defenders inflicted a loss upon the Maráthás of nearly 700 men, yet out of eight British officers (including two surgeons) there were five killed and wounded, and of a force of barely 800 men, more than a third, 271, were reckoned among the casualties upon that memorable occasion [1].

Smith reached the scene of the action on the 3rd, and followed the Peshwá on the 8th, who, having again passed close to Poona, pushed to the south, where he fell in with Pritzler. The latter now took up the chase, and pursued the enemy towards Gokák, but General Munro having hastily collected a small force to guard the line of the Gatpurba river, Bájí Ráo, too faint-hearted to fight, was obliged to turn in another direction. Moving rapidly, he now doubled

[1] Blacker, p. 179. In Appendix I of this work, p. 457, will be found Captain Staunton's modest report of his gallant action.

again, and shaking himself clear of Smith and Pritzler, who were both at his heels, he got to Sholápur by the end of January, not much the worse for his hurried flight, and having only lost a small part of his troops in rear-guard skirmishes. Here he was joined by the broken bands of Apá Sáhib's horse, who after their defeat at Nágpur marched across the Nizám's dominions and reached the Peshwa in safety.

The plan hitherto adopted by the British commanders had been unprofitable. Encumbered with long trains of baggage, supplies, and guns, they imposed great fatigue upon their troops by arduous marches, and failed to reach an active enemy who was everywhere at home in his dominions, and who moved with little to arrest his progress [1]. It was therefore determined, on the suggestion of Mr. Elphinstone, to proceed on a more rational principle; the two divisions were accordingly brought together, and a lightly equipped column was formed therefrom, prepared to make rapid marches, while the remainder was constituted into a force destined to undertake the reduction of the numerous strongholds that studded the south-west of India, and to bring about the regular military occupation of the country. Waiting till Pritzler should join him, Smith summoned Sátára, which surrendered on the 11th February.

[1] The pursuit entailed severe marches. The 4th Deccan Division covered 300 miles between the 22nd November and the 17th December (26 days); the Reserve, 346 miles between the 3rd and 27th January (25 days).—Blacker, p. 177, 190 and 283.

Meanwhile Lord Hastings had come to a decision of no small importance to the future history of British India, which materially contributed to the final pacification of the territories so long misgoverned by the Peshwá. Elphinstone having reported Bájí Ráo's defection in November, made two propositions on the policy to be followed when that prince should be subdued; one, his reinstatement as nominal ruler with reduced authority, and the other, his deposition and the elevation of a member of his family to the *Masnad* in his stead. Lord Hastings rejected both these alternatives, and came to the conclusion, in December, that the office and authority of the Peshwá were to be abolished and his territories annexed to the Company's possessions.

He was urged to this decision by many considerations. Bájí Ráo had for several years evinced a spirit of inveterate hostility which no treaty could repress nor moderation conciliate; a secret and redoubtable power belonged to the recognised chief of the Maráthá confederacy, placing him in a position which was at once a menace to British interests and a rallying-point to the discontented. Nor did this authority depend upon the extent of territory he ruled, for it originated in the office he held as Peshwá, and as long as he retained it, little hope remained for a permanent settlement in his dominions or where his suzerainty was acknowledged. It was obviously impossible to curtail this influence by treaties or by force, so too would it be futile to transfer it to any prince of the Peshwá's family. The only permanent solution was to uproot a dangerous growth altogether from Maráthá soil; and such a step, while it would avert future difficulties, would also serve as a wholesome object-lesson of British power, and show what minor chiefs might expect when their foremost prince had not been spared.

It was further decided to set up a new head for the Maráthá nation, and the ruler selected for this dignity was the representative of Sivají, Núr Náráyan, Rájá of Sátára. His new position was to be maintained by a respectable principality, but his independence was to be limited and his ambition restrained by suitable checks. It was hoped that by the resuscitation of old traditions in a safe form, the natives would be conciliated, and the name of the Peshwá forgotten, and that the descendant of the founder of the Maráthá empire would be as useful to British security in the south of India as the Mughal Emperor had been in the north.

This policy was published in a proclamation issued by Elphinstone upon the fall of Sátára[1], who was appointed Commissioner to carry it into execution and was vested with large discretionary powers as to details. The Peshwá was thus deposed and declared an outlaw; but he was still at large and in arms, he had hitherto baffled pursuit, and, more important than all, he retained as prisoner in his camp

[1] A translation of this Proclamation issued in the Maráthí language is to be found in Blacker, Appendix O, p. 462.

the very prince who formed such an important factor in the new arrangements which the Governor-General had determined to adopt.

Fortune, however, soon placed the Rájá of Sátára in British hands. General Smith tracked Bájí Ráo with a light column, and having fortunately come upon him unexpectedly at Ashti, on the 20th, he immediately attacked him with a body of horse. The Peshwá, as usual when danger was near, consulted his personal safety by galloping off from the field, and left his general, Gokla, to cover his retreat and the removal of the baggage. A sharp cavalry action ensued, in which the enemy was not only put to flight and his camp taken, but Gokla was killed and Núr Náráyan recovered. This reverse was a serious blow to the fugitive, and many of his adherents wavered in their allegiance and deserted his standard; but next to the loss of the Sátára Rájá, the death of his general was the worst disaster he experienced. Gokla had been a firm supporter of British interests in the past, and had done good service in the second Maráthá war at the beginning of the century; he was deeply indebted to the Supreme Government not only for his position at the Peshwá's court, but also for his life and possessions, frequently threatened by that capricious prince; by the latter, indeed, he had been treated with the most degrading contumely, but nevertheless he became in the end his devoted follower and ardent defender. By his death, Bájí Ráo lost an enterprising and energetic military leader, and was obliged afterwards to conduct his own military operations, as on no one else could he place any reliance[1].

He now directed his steps northwards to Khándesh, receiving near Násik the remnants of Holkar's forces and some few Pindárís, who having been defeated escaped pursuit; he was making for Burhámpur, in the hopes of reaching Sindhia, when he heard of the approach of Sir T. Hislop; thereupon he turned south, but, afraid of meeting Smith's division, he again altered his course and marched to the east (middle of March), in order to join the Bhonsla Rájá, whose subjects were represented to him as ripe for insurrection, and whose territories would therefore offer the best asylum in his present distress. This determination was brought about by affairs at Nágpur, and to these we must now briefly refer.

Apá Sáhib was no sooner restored to liberty early in January, as has already been recorded, than he sought for means to throw off the yoke which his perfidy had imposed upon him. His power of directing secret hostilities was still considerable, despite the diminution of his public authority, and it was soon ascertained that an Arab force was being collected at Chándá, and a depôt established there, for future operations against the British Government; added to this, he treacherously ordered his feudatories and Killadars to prosecute the war which he had engaged to relinquish, and to hold the forts which he had bound himself to surrender. Evidence of his duplicity

[1] Prinsep, ii. 183.

and unalterable hostility did not fail, and the danger it gave rise to was increased by the reports that Bájí Ráo had left his own dominions and was marching at the head of a strong army to Chándá to effect a junction with the scattered fragments of the Bhonsla's forces. There was every intention of carrying the war into Nágpur, and Mr. Jenkins, who had early applied to Lord Hastings for instructions, resolved that it would be imprudent to wait any longer, and acting upon his own responsibility he made Apá Sáhib a prisoner, and lodged him for safe custody in the Residency, until the Governor-General should decide upon his future treatment (15th March).

General Smith, who had only delayed in the south to conduct Núr Náráyan to Sátára, there to receive investiture from the Supreme Government at the hands of the Commissioner, marched to the north, and halting for a short time at Sirúr, left that place on the 10th March. Shortly afterwards, he heard of Bájí Ráo's eastward march, and concerting a plan of pursuit with Doveton, the two divisions followed, the latter taking a northerly route to prevent an irruption into Hindustán, the former moving along the Godávari river to anticipate any attempt in the direction of Haidarábád. About the same time Sir T. Hislop, preparing to give up his command in the Deccan according to the orders already referred to, the division he commanded was broken up and incorporated with the forces operating against the enemy. At the beginning of April, Bájí Ráo, who had marched unopposed towards Chándá with the utmost speed, wasting the Nizám's territory as he passed along, was heard of on the Wardhá river not far from its confluence with the Pengangá, where he hoped to receive support from the Bhonsla, and some alleviation of the fate that gave him no rest. But a great disappointment was in store for him, and instead of finding Apá Sáhib ready to join him, he was again entangled in the net which the British authorities had woven round him, and through which he was unable to break.

Adams now appears on the scene again; it has been mentioned that that commander had been detained near Bhopál, and it was intended that he should soon return to Hoshangábád, the usual station of the Nágpur subsidiary force; but Jenkins, having received early notice of Maráthá plans, recalled him promptly to meet the enemy. He reached Hinganghát on the 6th of April, in time to perform this service, as the ex-Peshwá had been previously delayed by the Nágpur Brigade which was sent out to oppose his advance upon Chándá. Bájí Ráo now heard with dismay of Apá Sáhib's imprisonment, and found himself hemmed in by British forces; his object was entirely frustrated, for, far from receiving any support, he had no hopes of even maintaining himself in the field till the rains fell, when military operations would have to be suspended; he therefore halted between the Wardhá and the Pengangá, in a state of dejection and irresolution. Adams, sure of his prey, waited until he had brought up his supplies, and received information of the approach of Doveton and Smith; he then attacked the enemy at Seoní, on the 17th of April. They made no stand whatsoever, and while they lost as many as 1,000 men, they only succeeded in wounding two sepoys; Bájí Ráo, as was his wont, headed the fugitives, who scattered wildly in all directions, some to the south-west, pursued by Smith, and others with their chief, followed by Doveton; the rout was complete, and nearly two-thirds of a numerous army are said to have deserted immediately afterwards. Doveton, however, unfortunately got on the track of a wrong body of the flying enemy, and failed to overtake the Peshwá, who on reaching the Tápti river turned northwards to endeavour, as a last and forlorn hope, to find an asylum in Sindhia's territories, and to secure the adhesion of that prince to his desperate cause. Adams remained behind and reduced Chándá in May, after which he returned to quarters at Hoshangábád.

Bájí Ráo did not however improve his position by this move, for his passage to the north was barred by forts in British possession, and by arrangements made by Sir J. Malcolm on the Narbadá. Added to this, he was being surrounded on all sides by the concentration of other troops in the neighbourhood, and Lord Hastings, hearing of his attempt to carry the war into Sindhia's country, was about to order Ochterlony to throw himself between the enemy and Gwalior, and to assume the direction of affairs in this quarter. Hemmed in all round, and brought to bay, the Peshwá's only chance of finding a refuge was in the stronghold of Asírgarh, where the Killadar was entirely at his service; but he quailed at the idea of a siege, and recognised that even there he would be by no means secure; accordingly he sent to Malcolm and offered to surrender if suitable terms were forthcoming. The latter had been Political Officer in the Deccan and was generally aware of the Governor-General's intentions regarding the Poona state, but his mission was over, and he was ignorant of the full details of the new arrangements. Believing, however, that it was supremely important to capture a prince who had so long eluded the efforts of the numerous troops employed against him, he took upon himself the responsibility of communicating with him, and of delaying the military operations by which he was to be surrounded. Negotiations began, and after a show of resistance, Bájí Ráo submitted and gave himself up, upon the assurance that he and his followers would be well treated, and that an annual pension of eight lakhs of rupees (£80,000) would be allotted for his personal support. From this moment this worthless ruler disappears from Indian history, and thenceforward he lived and died at Cawnpur, in captivity. He left no issue, but his heir was his adopted son, the infamous Náná Sáhib, whose evil career during the Indian Mutiny is well known, and requires no comment here.

Lord Hastings confirmed this capitulation in all its articles, but he signified his disapproval at its conclusion. His indignation had been justly aroused against Bájí Ráo, who 'had the villainy to send a secret offer of poisoning Gokla, the general of his army, if in consequence we would admit him to terms[1].' He had also wished to impress the natives of India by the capture of the Peshwá, without being forced to grant beforehand any conditions whatsoever, and he considered that the sum of money allotted for the maintenance of such a man was altogether too large. He had fixed two lakhs as the proper amount, believing that any surplus would be used to foment intrigues against the British authority. On the other hand, Malcolm pleaded that the Peshwá if driven to desperation would have taken refuge in Asírgarh, that it was impossible at that period of the year to besiege it, that as long as Bájí Ráo remained at large there would be no peace in the Deccan, and that the war would have been needlessly protracted for several months.

Lord Hastings was not convinced by this reasoning; but he acknowledged the importance of the capture, and 'the zeal and ability manifested by Sir J. Malcolm,' and stated in 1822, 'Now, after the lapse of four years from the period of Bájí Ráo's surrender, I am happy to state that none of the ill consequences I apprehended, from the very favourable terms offered by Sir J. Malcolm, have taken place, except that perhaps a larger actual expense has been incurred than would have sufficed to put him down. On reviewing the whole transaction, however, I see no reason for admitting that my original view, based on the facts before stated, was erroneous[2].'

[1] Private Journal, ii. 276.

[2] Malcolm's *Hist. of India*, i. 531; see also p. 518, &c., and App. No. V.

While Bájí Ráo was being pursued, the regular conquest of his dominions was undertaken by several columns of British troops. Towards the end of April, the whole tract of country lying between Sátára and Khándesh, as well as the Konkan, were occupied, and the numerous strongholds that guarded these districts reduced. Pritzler having completed the task assigned to him by the beginning of the month, marched to the south to join General Munro, whose operations must be briefly alluded to. That distinguished officer had been engaged in the autumn of 1817 in carrying out the stipulations of the treaty of Poona in the south of the Peshwá's dominions; appointed to the command of the Deccan Reserve Division, he found that there was much to be done in the districts where he was stationed, and he temporarily placed General Pritzler at the head of the force. The departure of the division left him almost without any troops, having at his disposal only six companies, a few troops of cavalry, and a small battering train; but he speedily reinforced these meagre resources by levies drawn from the inhabitants, and such was his personal character that, in spite of his military weakness, he effected by the end of January the conquest of the whole country up to the Malpurbi river, and defeated a Pindárí band, which, eluding capture in the north, penetrated to a point near Dhárwár. On being now slightly reinforced, he advanced northwards, occupying the country up to Belgáum, and taking that stronghold early in April. The strain upon the small column which had already accomplished so much, now impaired its efficiency, and Munro was powerless to continue his victorious advance, until Pritzler joined him; he then had a force of 4,000 men under him, with which he pushed to Sholápur, to undertake the reduction of that important fort. Sholápur, the Peshwá's principal military depôt, was garrisoned by 1,000 men, and was covered by an army of 6,000 Maráthás, of whom 1,200 were Arabs; notwithstanding the resistance of this army, the enemy were very soon put to flight (10th of May), and the town carried by escalade, the citadel falling five days later. This event completed the conquest of the south of the Peshwá's dominions.

In the north, the invasion of Khándesh began in the middle of May, before Doveton and Smith had returned from their chase after Bájí Ráo. It was more than ordinarily desirable to subdue that province, since it was the home of the Arabs,—a turbulent people who not only supported the Maráthás, but promoted disorder for its own sake; in some respects they were not unlike the Patháns, for having established themselves in the country they usurped all authority, tyrannised over the inhabitants, and opposed the introduction of even the semblance of regular government. Málegáon, the principal stronghold in the district, was the point to which the first military operations were directed, and its reduction proved a more difficult task than was at first anticipated. It was not until the 14th of June,—the enemy's magazine having blown up,—that the garrison capitulated; but on the fall of that fort, the whole province surrendered, and by the middle of June it may be said that all the ex-Peshwá's armies were defeated, his dominions, forts, and military depôts occupied, and the conquered country transferred by force of arms to the authority of the British Government.

Of all the numerous enemies banded against the British power in November, 1817, there remained in little more than six months, only one who was still at large, and Lord Hastings was not long in deciding his fate. The hostility evinced by Apá Sáhib in the spring of 1818, after what had already taken place at Nágpur, could not again be pardoned, and it was resolved to depose him; but, unlike the Peshwá, his office was not to be abolished, and a successor was found in the person of a child, Bájí Ráo Bhonsla, nephew of Pursají and son of the latter's sister. It was further ascertained about this time, that Apá Sáhib had been deeply concerned in the murder of the unfortunate Pursají, and in order to place the culprit in safe custody while the war lasted, it was arranged to send him to the fort of Allahábád. He left for this destination on the 3rd of May; but some of the native soldiers of his escort were bribed, and the ex-Rájá, having dressed himself up as an ordinary sepoy, contrived by their assistance to escape, and marched out of the camp in safety. It was usual for the Indian princes to have their limbs rubbed at night; upon this occasion a cushion had been prepared, and when the officer whose duty it was to visit the prisoner every two hours, came to his tent, he saw two servants engaged in this operation and was quite satisfied that his charge was in his keeping. Thus ample time was given to effect a successful escape, and Apá Sáhib made such good use of the respite, which his devoted followers had procured for him, that, in spite of every exertion made for his re-capture, he was not to be found and all trace of the fugitive was lost. His flight was of no real importance, and indeed it furnished an excuse for the pacification of certain districts which but for this event might have been left alone until a more favourable opportunity should present itself; but it necessarily protracted the war somewhat longer than otherwise would have been the case.

Apá Sáhib was harboured by some discontented natives living near Betúl, and round his standard there flocked a motley array of the broken fragments of Arabs and of the Maráthá states, and composed of the discordant elements they contained, now united by the common danger that threatened them all. In July they succeeded in cutting to pieces a small British detachment, and later they occasioned the deployment of Adams' force; but the rains interfered with military operations, and nothing decisive could be effected until the following year (1819), when the disturbed district was reduced to order and the enemy attacked. Apá Sáhib, whose energy in collecting an army far surpassed his courage in using it, was able to raise a respectable number of troops, but having no strongholds or depôts to rely on, and fearful of the consequences of the struggle he had challenged, he arranged with the Killadar of Asírgarh to give him shelter in that fort. He soon made for this refuge, and reached it in safety, accompanied by the Pindárí chief Chítu; but the Killadar, though he had no hesitation in receiving a Maráthá prince, was afraid to harbour a Pindárí, and the wretched man, rejected in the hour of danger and betrayed by false allies for their own most selfish advantage, was in consequence destroyed in the manner which has been already related.

Lord Hastings rightly judged that the ex-Bhonsla would fly for protection to Asírgarh, and while directing that in this event the Killadar was to be treated as a rebel, assembled a large force from the divisions of Malcolm, Doveton, and Adams, consisting of fifteen battalions, four regiments of cavalry, and a battering train, to reduce this formidable stronghold. The siege began on the 17th of March, 1819, and on the 9th of the following month the Killadar capitulated, when it was ascertained that his resistance was due to secret and pressing directions given by Sindhia himself, entirely at variance with the public declarations of that prince, who professed anxiety, and had issued orders that the fort should be surrendered in accordance with the treaty of Gwalior. Apá Sáhib also had again escaped and was nowhere to be found; but his power for mischief was now gone for ever, for every place was subdued, and further shelter there was none. An offer of a pension of two lakhs of rupees and a residence in British territory, on similar terms to those given to the ex-Peshwá, failed to receive any response, and he was at last heard of in exile in the Punjab, where Ranjít Singh tolerated his presence but refused to countenance him. Later, he was allowed to live in Rájputána under surveillance, and there he died without giving further trouble to the British Government.

Long before the capture of Asírgarh, which was the concluding military event of the last Maráthá war, Trimbakjí and other leaders of disorder were taken, and the former was again imprisoned in punishment for the Shástrí's murder, which he perpetrated in 1815. As peace was now everywhere restored, it is time to return to the arrangements which were made for the re-settlement of the provinces where hostilities had taken place.

CHAPTER VIII

RECONSTRUCTION IN CENTRAL INDIA AND IN THE SOUTH-WEST, 1818–1823

THERE is probably no period in the history of British progress in the East more full of interest and more fruitful of important consequences to India than that which has just been described, beginning in the autumn of 1817 and ending in the following June, when the war practically came to a conclusion. In that short space of time stupendous changes had taken place in the vast tracts of country where independent native rule prevailed, and the whole continent, bounded on the north-west by the Sutlej, was summarily brought into subjection to the Government of Calcutta [1]. The predatory system was finally stamped out, and the Maráthá Empire for ever crushed; everywhere victory crowned the efforts of the Governor-General, and though the military power of his enemies was contemptible, yet their latent force of resistance was considerable, and it was due to his foresight and

[1] Lord Hastings appears dazzled by the extraordinary alteration so suddenly effected in Central India, and declares in February, 1818, that he was 'still too near it to comprehend it thoroughly.' Private Journal, ii. 277.

vigour that his policy had been successful and his results decisive.

'What I contemplated,' he says in 1820, when describing his operations, 'was the pushing forward, unexpectedly, several corps which should occupy positions opposing insuperable obstacles to the junction of the army of any state with that of another; and even expose to extreme peril any sovereign's attempt to assemble the dispersed corps of his forces within his own dominions, should we see cause to forbid it. The success of this plan depended on the secrecy with which the preparations could be made, the proper choice of points to be seized, and the speed with which we could reach the designated stations[1].'

It is impossible not to admire the manner in which the plan was executed, and how carefully prepared it had been in every detail to effect the object for which it was intended. Though no blow was struck, Sindhia, when he least expected it, was isolated from the very outset of the campaign, and was obliged, much against his will, to maintain a neutral attitude. Amír Khán was in the same way separated from his allies, intimidated, and forced to disarm. The important line of the Narbadá being rapidly seized and firmly held, the native states of the Deccan were divided from those of Hindustán, and a good central position obtained, whence to operate with ease to the north and south. British forces were also interposed between Poona and Nágpur, and all co-operation between the princes of those states rendered impossible. And, lastly, the

[1] Malcolm's *Hist. of India*, i. 491. Summary, &c., p. 14.

Pindárís were effectually surrounded, deprived of support, hunted down, and destroyed. The preliminary dispositions having been made with much forethought and skill, the results anticipated followed as a matter of course; so when the Peshwá and the Bhonsla Rájá revolted, they found themselves surrounded and their provinces quickly overrun, Holkar was met and easily defeated, and the rest were overawed and rendered incapable of offering resistance. Every contingency had been amply provided for; the Maráthá states were powerless to combine when they most required mutual assistance, and the hordes of freebooters were unable to derive the smallest benefit from those native princes who were anxious to give them support.

The policy adopted to put down disorder, though it ended by a large accession of territory in India, was not intended to add to British possessions; on the contrary, the operations undertaken were purely of a defensive nature, and had for their object the protection of the Company's dominions and the safety of British subjects and allies. Lord Hastings repudiated distinctly any aggressive design, and in 1820 communicated his views on this subject to England in the following words:—

'But for the unforeseen perfidy and unaccountable folly of the Peshwá and the Rájá of Nágpur, I might have congratulated myself and your Honourable Company on the successful accomplishment of my original hope of effecting the suppression of the predatory system, without disturbing any of the established powers of India, or adding a rood to the possession of the British Government. I feel assured your Honourable Committee has been satisfied that such was my earnest desire; and that its disappointment has been occasioned by circumstances beyond my control. When those circumstances did occur, and the necessity arose for my directing your arms against treacherous allies and declared enemies, you will, I am persuaded, admit the impracticability of my adhering to those limits which my duty and inclination would otherwise have prescribed, without a sacrifice of your interest and security which no profession of obedience to orders, issued under a different view of things, would have justified to myself or my country [1].'

But the war nevertheless did occasion a destructive period in India, and extended over a far wider area than was represented by the territories of these two Maráthá rulers. No independent state had escaped its disturbing effects, the whole balance of power had been violently shaken and completely upset, and constitutional changes of a far-reaching and fundamental character had been made in many provinces. A comprehensive scheme of reconstruction had therefore to be effected, and as the territories to be submitted to this process extended over nearly half a million square miles, the task was a gigantic one, and entailed a greater and more important labour by far than that which had hitherto occupied the energies of the Governor-General. By the results he achieved is his success to be commended or his failure blamed; for easy as it often is to abolish an evil system, its destruction is

[1] Malcolm's *Hist. of India*, i. 502.

mis-spent labour, unless it is replaced by something better and more useful to the interests of mankind.

Nor was it only the right of conquest that imposed upon the Indian Government the duty of a re-settlement of the disturbances which hostilities had created, for the immediate and natural result of the war was the *de facto* recognition, by the whole of India, of England's supreme suzerainty; and although that position was not assumed *de jure* until within our own generation (some sixty years after the events we are now recording), yet none the less did British authority everywhere supplant the Mughal Emperor effectually and conclusively, and the natives of India universally acknowledged that his traditional rights had thenceforward passed away irrevocably into the keeping of the Government of Calcutta. There was consequently an almost moral as well as material force at the back of the Government, and while this contributed to make the work to be undertaken easier than might otherwise have been the case, yet it also added in no small degree to the responsibility incurred, that the reconstruction to be brought about should be equitable, satisfactory, and beneficial to the people whose happiness and future welfare was entrusted to the care of the British nation.

In the work of pacification (a description of which must necessarily be exceedingly brief and cursory in this small volume), Lord Hastings had the good fortune to be assisted by some of the most distinguished Anglo-Indian administrators that have ever served in the East. In a long roll of British statesmen, whose labours in the public service of India have trained the natives to habits of order and civilization, and conciliated the people to higher ideas and to Western rule, few stand more prominent than Elphinstone, Munro, Malcolm, Metcalfe, and Ochterlony. These men and others, who served in a minor but scarcely less important capacity, were all remarkable for their ability and for their thorough knowledge of native affairs, as well as for their active sympathy with the prejudices and sentiments of the people with whom they came into contact. Their efforts upon this occasion were conspicuously successful, and contributed in no small degree to make the reconstruction durable and advantageous not only to the conquerors but also to the inhabitants.

To secure the future and permanent tranquillity of the Indian continent, it is evident that the paramount authority of England had to be asserted and maintained over the foreign affairs of all the native states, and this included the control of their military concerns. This principle was everywhere adopted and enforced. But the existing order which had prevailed in the internal affairs of the various states was disturbed as little as possible, and only such territory added to the Company's direct possession as was necessary to establish securely British power, or which could not be otherwise settled. As an example of this, the ex-Peshwá's dominions were taken over and placed under English administration, in conformity with the policy which was adopted in the Poona principality, and for reasons which have already been explained in the last chapter. But elsewhere the general rule which prevailed was to incorporate that territory alone whose revenues were sufficient to maintain the subsidiary forces which were required for the control of the native princes. Society was left free and unfettered to develop itself, without the imposition, by force or interference, of a higher culture for which it was unfitted, and the rulers who were still preserved at the head of their states were made independent, as far as it was consistent with the central control of Calcutta to be exercised for the preservation of general tranquillity.

It was further determined to increase the influence of those states where intelligent chiefs existed,—native princes who co-operated with British officers in the introduction of salutary reforms, and who, having deserved consideration at the hands of the Governor-General for the services they rendered, would be likely to lay the foundation of civilized government in the provinces under their rule. It was natural that they should be rewarded and encouraged; and there was plenty of land at the disposal of Lord Hastings to carry out this principle, for many worthless chiefs were dispossessed or their territories reduced.

In effecting these changes, and indeed on other occasions, an endeavour was moreover made to remove all future causes of contention, and with this object, to define the boundaries which hitherto existed between the various states, and which, being hopelessly involved and indeterminate, were a fruitful source of bloodshed and anarchy. To give some idea of the confusion which existed in this respect, it may be mentioned that many of the Maráthá princes had rights over one and the same village, and not unfrequently did it occur that portions of a distant town, unconnected territorially with either of its sovereigns, were ruled by one chief and the remainder by another[1]. Causes of dispute were therefore constantly at hand to produce among a turbulent people perennial feuds and unnecessary disturbances, and hence it became imperative that a new delimitation of rights and frontiers should at once be made by the paramount authority, to obviate for the future so extraordinary an invitation to discord. An example of this strange Maráthá system, which was incompatible with the rudiments of civil government, and the occasion of feuds and riot, is given by Lord Hastings:—

'The radical policy of the Maráthás was oddly avowed lately by an agent of Sindhia. The rights or possessions of the Maráthá chiefs are strangely intermixed with those of the different Rájás between the Jumna and the Narbadá. In one instance there was a district enveloped in the territories of the Rájá of Búndi, the annual revenue of which was

[1] A statement of Holkar's various claims is given in Wilson, viii. Appendix vi, showing how Maráthá rights were so inextricably intermixed that anarchy was the inevitable result.

divisible in equal portions between the latter chief, Holkar, and Sindhia. As the two Maráthá princes kept agents there to watch over their shares, there was an obvious chance of quarrels; and we wished to secure the Búndi chief, who had been taken under our protection, against any vexatious pretension on the part of his neighbours. It was therefore proposed that Sindhia should cede his title to any income from the district in question, and should receive from us certain villages producing a rent considerably beyond what we wished him to give up. A strong disinclination to close with this proposal was manifested. When it was urged that Sindhia would not only be a pecuniary gainer by the exchange, but that he would acquire a tract which actually connected itself with his old possessions, and would be exclusively his, the Maráthá negotiator denied that the circumstance of sole occupancy could be an advantage to his master equal to what the Mahárájá enjoyed by his co-partnership in the Búndi district. On surprise being expressed at this assertion, he explained it by saying, "We Maráthás have a maxim that it is well to have a finger in every man's dish." His meaning was, that there was solid value in pretexts for interference which would afford opportunities of pillage or extortion[1].'

Finally, it was hoped, by the creation or development of states not likely to co-operate with the Maráthás, that the intrigues of the latter would be paralysed and their ambition kept in check. With this object some of the Muhammadan princes were strengthened and their dominions enlarged.

To sum up the general principles which were adopted in effecting the reconstruction of native India, conquered by Lord Hastings in the third and

[1] Private Journal, ii. 330. Summary, &c., p. 24.

last Maráthá war, we may quote a short paragraph taken from a work which appeared in 1825[1]:—

'The system which prevails throughout is pretty uniform. There is, first, a native family vested with the nominal sovereignty; then there is a military force essentially British, having British officers, or there is a British cantonment at no great distance, and sometimes both, to assure the submission of the population to whatever may be ordained. For the application of this force, and to watch over the conduct of those who originate the administrative measures, there is everywhere a British Political Agent or Resident, reporting only to his government, and receiving his orders thence, but exercising a large personal discretion as to interference or non-interference with the native local authority.'

It has been already mentioned that British protection was accepted in 1817 by Nasír Muhammad, Nawáb of Bhopál, and that he faithfully maintained his engagements; moreover, he co-operated usefully with Colonel Adams in arranging for the submission of many of the Pindárís, and the measures he adopted tamed those brigands and colonised some of his waste lands. His good will was rewarded by increase of territory, so that the little state rose to political importance in Málwá, and acquired a revenue sufficient to maintain a high position and to exercise a considerable influence in Central India. Nasír Muhammad, the enlightened Nawáb, was accidentally killed in November, 1819, and the Supreme Government having to intervene, settled the succession. It will

[1] Prinsep, ii. 407.

be recollected that the neighbouring principality of Ságar was occupied by British troops; as a special concession, the detachment stationed there was allowed to take the place of a subsidiary force in Bhopál.

The districts ceded to British authority in the valley of the Narbadá (formerly under various native princes), were placed under the management of a Commissioner in 1818, with orders to disturb the customs which prevailed there as little as possible. Later, in 1827, Ságar was added to the province so formed, and under this administration, the revenues rose slightly from twenty-two lakhs of rupees in 1818, to twenty-six in 1839[1].

The settlement of Rájputána was quite as important as that of Málwá, for the predatory system had caused equally disastrous effects, and the perpetual strife it engendered, as well as the constant feuds which raged between the different factions in that locality, were fatal to public order. The pacification of this turbulent district was entrusted to Mr. Metcalfe, the Resident at Delhi, who was ably assisted by Captain Tod, and in 1819, on Metcalfe's appointment as Political Secretary, Sir D. Ochterlony discharged his difficult duties. The Resident was instructed to demand that the tributes which had been irregularly levied from the Rájput princes by Maráthá and Pathán chiefs, should for the future be paid to the Supreme Government, in return for which protection was to be given on the usual conditions, viz.

[1] Wilson, viii. 400.

that no alliances were to be entered into with other states, and that all disputes were to be referred to British arbitration; he was further directed to abolish the traditional suzerainty which had been technically enjoyed by the Mahárání of Udaipur,—a prince whose real weakness had caused great disorder by the misrule which military violence had produced everywhere, and which he was totally unable to check. According to the new system all the Rájput Rájás were put on an equal footing, that is, they were placed under a protected dependence on British supremacy, and it was hoped, as soon as they were subjected to the suzerainty exercised at Calcutta, that hereditary jealousies would be appeased and the predatory gangs rendered impossible for the future.

Protective treaties were concluded with the Rájás of Kotah, Jodhpur, Udaipur, Búndi, Jaipur, and with many others, and the disputes which some of these princes had with their Thákurs, or vassals, were adjusted. Affairs in Jaipur, however, were not easily arranged, and in May, 1818, Sir D. Ochterlony was obliged to undertake the reduction of two forts, which speedily submitted and disposed the more turbulent feudatories to come to terms. But in the following December, Jagat Singh, the Rájá, died, and leaving no heir, a contest was imminent: though this disaster was happily avoided by the birth of a posthumous child, yet anarchy continued to flourish, and it was not until 1823 that Ochterlony could introduce peace into the distracted principality. The other Rájput states proved to be more easily managed, and although the British Government had occasionally to intervene, the effects of the new system were gradually felt, reforms were undertaken, feuds came to an end, and the turbulence of the Thákurs was restrained.

'I have only to add,' writes Sir D. Ochterlony, when reporting officially to the Supreme Government, 'that throughout my tour I have derived the most sincere gratification, from observing the prevalent tranquillity and increasing prosperity of the country. From the prince to the peasant, I have found every tongue eloquent in the expression of gratitude to the British Government for the blessings they enjoy. Discontent or oppression appears equally unknown, except at Ujjain, and a few other places in the immediate occupancy of Sindhia's relatives [1].'

The extraordinary folly of the Peshwá and the Bhonsla Rájá in provoking a quarrel with the British Government, stands out conspicuously as one of the inexplicable events in the history of this period. Constantly plotting against the power with which they affected to be in alliance, and to whose influence they owed their positions, they seemed incapable of adopting vigorous measures to throw off the yoke it imposed, or to perform the engagements it required. Destitute of real ability, even deficient in personal courage, they displayed none of the generosity which attracts sympathy, nor any of the qualities which might atone for their perfidy, and they fell as they deserved to fall,—unlike the many

[1] Summary, &c., p. 19, and Appendix B.

popular leaders who have been crushed in the defence of national rights,—unlamented, unhonoured, and forgotten. Nevertheless, at first their revolt had the approval of the whole of the Maráthá nation, and the confidence reposed in the wisdom and the plans of the native princes was sufficient to induce the almost universal belief among the Hindus that the English would be driven out of Asia. Nor were these expectations dissipated after the first defeats, and it was not until the victory at Ashti, which delivered the Rájá of Sátára from the Peshwá's power, that the natives acknowledged resistance to be vain [1].

Henceforward the treachery of the two Maráthá rulers in the Deccan became an advantage to the Governor-General; for the timidity of many was roused by the sudden and unexpected collapse of national aspirations, and they feared to lose their possessions if they obstinately maintained a hostile attitude towards the winning side; the intelligence of others soon perceived that their princes were contemptible, and not worth supporting; while to all was the weakness of the foremost Maráthá chiefs so clear, that the other states took warning by the example unfolded before their eyes. No real principle of national life was at stake in the contest, and if there had been such a thing, the conduct of the Maráthá chiefs soon dissipated the charm. Hence when the Peshwá surrendered, and when the power of a few tyrants was broken down, their authority

[1] Prinsep, ii. 288.

was gone and the glamour that belonged to their position disappeared.

Nor was it forgotten that British rule, where it existed, had been just and satisfactory, that native customs were maintained and respected, and that the Governor-General was the sole avenger of a Bráhman of rank who had been sacrificed by the Peshwá himself at the bidding of a low-caste adventurer.

Added to this, there was a general feeling current in India, that the supremacy of England was an event which was not to be resisted, and many natives of the better classes desired that British rule should be established. Numerous examples of this are given in the history of that time, to which we may add the following incidents mentioned in the Private Journal:—

The Ráj Guru, or high priest, of Nepál, thus expressed himself to the Assistant Resident at Khátmándu:—

'One after another the native sovereigns will be urged, by folly, or overweening pride, to attack you; and then you must, in self-defence, conquer; and then you are much the stronger, whether you intended it or not [1].'

And again, an English officer having asked a native whether it was really the wish of the people to see their country transferred to a foreign rule:—

'To be sure it is our wish,' replied the man. 'Can you

[1] Private Journal, ii. 206.

think us such fools as not to desire to have our estates and the earnings of our industry secure? We must always be exposed to the cupidity of a native sovereign; but we know that the British, either from a spirit of justice, or from policy, always leave individuals in the enjoyment of their property[1].'

In short, numerous causes contributed to form a sort of public opinion, as soon as the assured success of British arms gave it the power and the faculty to speak out without apprehension, and this opinion set in with increasing force against the leaders of the revolt. In this way the princes who survived destruction made efforts towards reform, and once they tried to introduce order; the benefits it afforded became apparent to their untutored minds, and a natural improvement in their affairs took place.

So strong were these influences, that they became immediately apparent even at the courts of Holkar and Sindhia, where, judging from what were the feelings there, we should least expect to find them operating. The treaty signed with Holkar at Mandesar, 6th January, 1818, has already been noticed. The prince, Málhár Ráo, was a minor, and through British influence Tántia Jogh was appointed minister, and was vested with the powers of regent. This arrangement, having been facilitated by the fact that the heads of this distracted state had been removed by internal feuds or by recent events, proved to be very satisfactory. Tántia Jogh was a man of

[1] Private Journal, i. 236.

no small ability and discretion, and of considerable education and character; he was instrumental in adjusting difficulties as they arose by his own authority, without resorting to British intervention—a course which was sometimes necessary, but which was discouraged and sparingly applied, and only followed in cases of extreme urgency. Under his guidance and by the advice and assistance of Sir J. Malcolm, the confusion existing in the principality was rapidly removed. It was, however, found impossible to separate, in any thoroughly satisfactory manner, Holkar's territories from those of Sindhia, with which they were interwoven in a very confused and in true Maráthá fashion, but the Resident was always present to smooth over and to arbitrate upon differences should they arise. By the treaty just mentioned, portions of Holkar's dominions north of Búndi and south of the Sátpura hills were ceded, and Múlhár Ráo renounced for ever the rights he arrogated to himself in Rájputána. In this manner his territories were considerably diminished, but on the other hand the principality was made more compact, and was easier to govern. As a result, the revenues which had been only four lakhs of rupees, raised with difficulty, amounted in 1826, when Tántia Jogh died, to as much as thirty-five lakhs[1].

The arrangement made with Sindhia in November, 1817, had been of a temporary character. Before dispersing the army which was watching him and

[1] Wilson, viii. 405.

insuring his good behaviour, it became necessary to conclude a permanent treaty with him in 1818. Sindhia practically forfeited no territory, but he agreed to certain exchanges of districts by which he was not the loser, and in this manner he ceded Ajmere to the British Government, a province which was much required to exclude Maráthá influence from Rájputána, and to maintain a restraining check over the affairs in that turbulent locality. When Daulat Ráo's duplicity with regard to Asírgarh became known (in 1819), Lord Hastings contented himself by sending the incriminating correspondence to Gwalior, with an intimation that the fort would be retained in perpetuity; but with politic moderation he made no further demands, and took no more notice of the incident. Since that time the attitude of the Mahárájá towards the English changed completely, and far from objecting to a proposal by which the command of a body of his troops was given to British officers, he willingly accepted a treaty in 1820, which, though not in name, was practically the same as a subsidiary alliance. Under this protection, he recovered many of the provinces which his insubordinate commanders had usurped, his finances which were in great disorder improved, and a system of regular government was soon introduced, which relieved the inhabitants of the crushing tyranny which oppressed them.

Nor was the feeling of resignation to British guidance exceptional in the north; in the Deccan also, the vassals of the revolted princes soon began to submit to the inevitable with cheerfulness and alacrity, when the Commissioner, Mr. Elphinstone, seizing the most suitable opportunity, issued the proclamation which announced the Peshwá's deposition in February, 1818. His action in this respect was made still more successful by the wise measures he took to reconcile all classes of society to the new system, first, by assuring the payers of taxes that Maráthá extortion was at an end; secondly, by the toleration, even protection, promised to the Bráhmans and to the religious institutions of the country; and, thirdly, by the security extended to the holders of fiefs, on condition that submission was made and that the rights of others were not interfered with. The numerous bands of military adventurers who throve under the ex-Peshwá's disorderly government alone remained dissatisfied; as many of these as possible, after they had been duly depressed by reverses in the field, were given suitable employment in the native levies, raised to serve in the provinces which had been transferred to the British Government. The danger that a great and sudden influx of Bájí Ráo's defeated forces would commit acts of plunder on their return home, was one which could not be overlooked, and extreme care was taken to meet such a contingency, by encouraging those that could not be drafted into the army, to settle down peaceably, and by severely dealing with marauders. These precautions were efficiently carried out, and it speaks well for Elphinstone's enlightened and vigorous administration, that the peace of the country was in no way disturbed. The Arabs, however, were treated in a different manner; they were disorderly aliens, most difficult to tame, and unless they changed their habits, there was no reason why they should be allowed to remain and disturb the Hindus who were beginning to settle down into peaceable pursuits; those, therefore, who could not be restrained, were made to leave the districts over which they had tyrannised, and were shipped off to their native country.

The dominions of the ex-Peshwá, except those portions handed over to native princes, were administered by British officers; Munro was retained in the south, settling the country beyond the Kistna river; the province of the Konkan was immediately added to the Bombay possessions, but the remainder was kept separate under Elphinstone, until he was appointed Governor, when the whole was transferred to that Presidency (1820). The Rájá of Sátára, though treated with the utmost deference, was more of a nominal sovereign than anything else; the principality was at first administered by an English officer (Captain Grant Duff); but in September, 1819, future relations were agreed to, under which the Rájá was still kept in a state of dependence but was given greater freedom of action than had been the case before; these arrangements came into operation in 1822.

We have seen that in the Nágpur state, which though extensive was not much more valuable than that of

Sátára, a child was placed on the *Masnad* instead of Apá Sáhib. Lord Hastings, who endeavoured as far as he could to abstain from all interference in the internal affairs of the native states, desired to set up a Hindu administration, but after a short experiment the plan failed, and for some years British officers had to carry on the government, under the Resident and in the name of the young Rájá. The Governor-General made continual efforts to form a native ministry and so relieve himself of a charge which he had unwillingly undertaken, and which was contrary to the general policy adopted in the unabsorbed provinces; but during his stay in India, this alteration was impossible, and the change was made later. It should, however, be added here that in order to secure entire control over the foreign affairs of the Bhonsla's dominions, his army was placed under British officers.

The re-settlement consequent upon the third Maráthá war extended also, but in a minor degree, to the states of Haidarábád and of Baroda, where hostilities had not disturbed the relations of the princes who reigned there with the Supreme Government. A re-adjustment of territory was subsequently made in the Nizám's dominions, and in 1822 that sovereign was relieved of the antiquated claims which the Peshwá had upon him, in the shape of 'chauth' or quarter revenues,—a form of tribute which, being irregularly levied and often resisted, led to interminable disputes, and was the cause of considerable trouble. The Nizám, moreover, received certain districts which, lying geographically near his own provinces, belonged formerly to Bájí Ráo, to the Bhonsla, and to Holkar; in return, he yielded territory of less value, with the result that his dominions were consolidated and his frontiers more accurately defined.

The Gáekwár of Baroda had already received considerable advantages by the treaty of Poona, June, 1817, amounting to an increased revenue of about twenty-two lakhs of rupees[1]. After the war, an exchange of territory was effected and an increase of the subsidiary force (to be paid for by the native prince) was agreed to. Relations with Baroda were somewhat complicated by the fact that the British Government had for many years practically ruled there, on account of the imbecility of the Gáekwár Anand Ráo. This prince died in 1819, and was succeeded by his brother, Syájí Ráo, and it then became necessary to enter upon a new agreement with that state. Mr. Elphinstone, on becoming Governor of Bombay, accordingly proceeded to Baroda and concluded a treaty in 1820, by which the control so long exercised over the Gáekwár was practically maintained, although the latter was now granted an increase of power over the internal affairs of his principality which could not formerly have been allowed.

Such generally were the main lines of the reconstruction effected in Central India and in the South-West, after one of the most decisive wars undertaken by

[1] Wilson, viii. 401.

Great Britain in Asia. As a result, about two-thirds of the Indian Continent was held under the direct management of the British Government, and in the newly acquired provinces, as had been the case in the older, an enlightened administration soon improved the face of the country and the lot of the inhabitants; the people speedily became reconciled to their new masters and to the civilisation they introduced. In the remaining third, native rulers governed, but subject to the vigilant and judicious control of the Supreme Government. It naturally took a longer time for an improvement to take place in these districts, but nevertheless a marked change for the better did shortly manifest itself. Villages which had been desolate and ruined were re-peopled, confidence was gradually restored, the wandering bands of military marauders and adventurers ceased, the revenues increased, and general prosperity was introduced. 'The dark age of trouble and violence,' says a writer of the day, already often quoted[1], 'which so long spread its malign influence over the fertile regions of Central India, has thus ceased from this time; and a new era has commenced, we trust, with brighter prospects,—an era of peace, prosperity, and wealth at least, if not of political liberty and high moral improvement.'

This prophecy has not been falsified, but it is not to be supposed that the new order which was established was a perfect work, and that it did not give rise to

[1] Prinsep, ii. 421.

future abuses which required correction. It is seldom that any reform can be final or complete in its operations, and if this is so in smaller affairs, how much the more must it not be the case in a gigantic work of reconstruction where misgovernment had existed for generations over an immense area of territory? The imperfections of the re-settlement were foreseen at the time, and while it was held that the general principles upon which it was based were the best that could be adopted, yet it was also allowed that they would require modifications in detail at no distant date. We have seen that the principles consisted in the following points, viz. that the native chiefs were left as free as possible in the administration of their internal affairs, but that they were absolutely restrained in their foreign relations, and that their military establishments were removed from their practical control. In time the system disclosed its defects, for the Indian princes too often neglected the duties of their own limited government, and far from ruling their subjects for the benefit of the people, tyrannised and oppressed them in an intolerable manner[1]. Such a shameless disregard of every principle of government when it occurred, could not but concern the paramount authority of England, and the consequences have been the further extension of British rule in a way which has been totally undesired by the supreme power. These events form no part of the present

[1] See Marquess of Dalhousie, *Rulers of India* series, by Sir W. Hunter, p. 125.

work, and have only been mentioned to show that while the reconstruction effected by Lord Hastings was satisfactory at the time, it formed but a step in the general development of English ascendency in India.

CHAPTER IX

FOREIGN RELATIONS; INTERNAL AFFAIRS; THE GREAT CASE OF PALMER & CO.

So much space has been necessarily taken up with the great questions which agitated Central India, that there is little room left in this short sketch of the administration of Lord Hastings to describe the other public transactions which took place during the period of his active rule. It is therefore only proposed to indicate a few of them as briefly as possible, dividing those that relate to foreign affairs from matters that concern internal policy, and thus to complete, it is hoped, a general view of the important events in the far East which took place at this time.

Without entering upon the details of the irritating disputes with which the Indian Government became involved with Burma, and which soon afterwards culminated in a war, it will perhaps be sufficient to mention here, that though Lord Hastings had considerable difficulty in maintaining peaceable relations with that country, yet he succeeded in doing so by the adoption of a firm and conciliatory attitude. He was exceedingly unwilling to provoke a quarrel, and during his time the Burmese had no reasonable cause for complaint. Nevertheless, such was their eagerness to avenge themselves on what they considered their wrongs, that they fulminated a declaration of war against the Supreme Government in 1818, when the Maráthá crisis had reached a climax; but they miscalculated their power, for before they could move, their allies had been subdued and they themselves had been defeated by the Siamese. The Governor-General accordingly put an end summarily to their arrogant pretension to destroy the British Empire in India, and 'evaded the necessity of noticing an insolent step' by treating the hostile message as a forgery[1].

It may be interesting to remark that Ceylon about this time (1818–19) was finally subjugated, and the whole island, with the assistance of Indian troops, placed under the British authority.

During Lord Minto's administration in India, the settlements in Java were conquered by an expedition from Bengal, but they were shortly afterwards (1814) restored to the Dutch, so unconditionally, that no provision was made to maintain the treaties which had been contracted with the native powers for the benefit of British trade. The Dutch immediately attempted to exclude all foreign competition in the archipelago, and had it not been for the activity of Sir Thomas Raffles (Governor of a small colony in Sumatra), their efforts would probably have been successful.

[1] Malcolm's *History of India*, i. 549, &c.; Private Journal, ii. 341; Summary, &c., p. 18.

Lord Hastings, judging that the question of opposing a European power was one which required reference to England, annulled Raffles' first measures, but he approved of the policy of counteracting the exclusion which was sought to be brought about, and expressed the following opinion—'that the proceedings of the Netherlands authorities since the arrival of the Commissioners-General to receive charge of the Dutch colonies, had been actuated by a spirit of ambition, by views of boundless aggrandisement and rapacity, and by a desire to obtain the power of monopolising the commerce of the eastern archipelago, and excluding the English from these advantages which they had long enjoyed, and which they only wished to share in common with the other nations of the earth.' He considered it necessary, therefore, to strengthen British possessions in the far East, and thus to secure a safe trade-route to China, which otherwise would have been closed. With this object, he approved of a proposition to occupy Singapore, which was then an almost desert island, inhabited only by a few fishermen. Raffles promptly put the plan into execution (1819), despite the protests of the Dutch, who did not contemplate any such operation. Considerable friction between the two powers was the result, until 1824, when a treaty was signed with Holland, by which certain territory was exchanged and the respective spheres of influence of the two countries were defined, giving England a secure passage for her merchandise, and leaving the legitimate aspirations of the Dutch free scope to develop. It may be added that about this time missions were sent to Siam and to Cochin China, to promote the expansion of British commerce in those regions, but little or no results followed these efforts at the time[1].

The security of trade in Asia was further established by the destruction of pirates, who from time immemorial infested the coasts of India and the approaches thereto. Several expeditions were fitted out for this purpose in 1819–20 to the Persian Gulf and to Arabia, and by the year 1822 the predatory fleets near the Indian shore from the Konkan to Cutch were suppressed, and the mischief they produced disappeared.

Returning to the continent of India, good relations were preserved all through Lord Hastings' administration with Ranjít Singh, the enlightened ruler of the Sikhs at Lahore. There was, however, a temporary difficulty with the Mírs of Sind, consequent upon affairs in Cutch which will be immediately noticed. The policy of the Governor-General was carefully to avoid all quarrels with tribes living beyond the Indus, as being quite outside the sphere of British operations. The differences with the Sind Mírs were adjusted by the moderation of the Bombay Government, November 1820, in a satisfactory and honourable manner, and peace was maintained on that frontier.

Affairs in Cutch had, however, been in disorder for

[1] Wilson, viii. 456, &c.

a long time; but as they did not affect British interests, there was no ground for interference, until 1813, when frequent raids were made across the Rann into protected territory. These marauding expeditions called for chastisement, and necessitated the partial subjugation of Cutch, which was not entirely accomplished until 1822, when it was finally incorporated into the Indian Empire, and placed under the control of the paramount authority of Calcutta.

The internal tranquillity of provinces under the direct rule of the Company was disturbed only slightly during the nine years of Lord Hastings' administration. Popular insurrections unfortunately took place at Bareilly and Cuttack in 1816 and 1817 respectively, which, though they caused much anxiety at the time, were put down without much difficulty. In the former case the cause of the disturbance was a reform which was hastily introduced in the collection of the police-tax, and appears to have arisen from mismanagement on the part of the local authority; in the latter case, where the discontent spread over a much wider area, the inhabitants had undoubted grievances, and it is satisfactory to be able to record that as soon as order was restored, fitting redress was applied, and the discontent was allayed.

The large landowners in the Doáb, called Tálukdárs, also gave some trouble about this time, to which allusion should be made. These local chiefs had been allowed to arrogate to themselves powers of sovereignty over their tenants which were oppressive and called for correction; protecting themselves by strong forts, and defying the central Government of Calcutta, they harboured gangs of banditti and disorganised the districts over which they had usurped an unjust authority. In the early part of 1817 Lord Hastings put an end to their depredations by the destruction of Háthras, the stronghold of the principal chief of the province, and the most formidable fortress in that part of India. The speedy reduction of the place was of considerable importance, for it was deemed to be impregnable by the natives, and a success of this kind was much wanted, 'to retrieve our military character in the article of sieges[1].' The remaining chieftains, after this, promptly submitted, and surrendered their forts, eleven in number, some of which were very strong, without any further resistance. All these works were then dismantled, the forces belonging to them were disbanded, and the Tálukdárs were allowed to retain in their service only a few armed attendants for the defence of their households[2]. In this way was peace re-established in the province; but as the incident illustrates the military ability of the Governor-General, and the reforms he introduced in the Company's armies, it will perhaps be interesting to add a few words upon the subject. We can best do this in Lord Hastings' own words:—

'One of my earliest military cares,' he writes in the Summary of his administration, just quoted, 'had been to satisfy

[1] Private Journal, ii. 182.

[2] Summary, &c., p. 13.

myself why we had made so comparatively unfavourable a display in sieges. The details at once unfolded the cause; it is well known that nothing can be more insignificant than shells thrown with long intervals; and we never brought forward more than four or five mortars where we undertook the capture of a fortified place. Hence, the bombardment was futile; so that at last the issue was to be staked on mounting a breach, and fighting hand to hand with a soldiery, skilful, as well as gallant, in defending the prepared intrenchments. This was not the oversight of the Bengal artillery officers, for no men can be better instructed in the theory, or more capable in the practice of their profession than they are; it was imputable to a false economy on the part of the Government. The outlay, in providing for the transportation of mortars, shells, and platforms, in due quantity, would certainly have been considerable; and it was on that account forborne. The miserable carriages of the country, hired for the purpose, where a military exertion was contemplated, were utterly unequal to the service, and constantly failed under the unusual weight, in the deep roads through which they had to pass. Therefore, we never sat down before a place of real strength furnished with the means which a proper calculation would have allotted for its reduction. Sensible of this injurious deficiency, I had with the utmost diligence instituted a transport train; and it was in reliance on its efficiency that I assured the Council of the short resistance which Háthras should offer. Expedition, no less than secrecy, was important, to prevent any interventions which might trouble us in the undertaking; and notwithstanding that the advance of the troops was so rapid, that the Tálukdár of Háthras had information of their approach only two days before the actual investment took place, forty-two mortars kept pace with the march of the force; and from the incessant shower of bombs, the garrison was unable to persist in defending the place more than fifteen hours[1].'

It will be remembered that the Indian Government was indebted to the Nawáb Wazír for the financial assistance he rendered during the Nepál war. Lord Hastings, whose inclinations led him to avoid interference in the internal affairs of native states, and who was specially disposed to treat this prince with the utmost forbearance, refrained from forcing reforms into Oudh, which were much needed, and contented himself with expostulations, which had no effect; a more rigorous course of action became necessary, but it was not adopted until the Governor-General had left India. The latter furthermore permitted the Nawáb to discard his old title of Wazír, or hereditary chief minister to the Mughal Emperor, for that of Padshah, or independent King of Oudh (1819), and sanctioned the change (which was not, however, to alter the relations subsisting between Lucknow and Calcutta), on the ground that it would benefit British interests, by dividing the Muhammadans among themselves, and by weakening the moral power of the house of Timúr, which nominally reigned at Delhi. The Nawáb's ambition was unfavourably received by his compeers, and when a similar dignity was offered to the Nizám, he rejected it, as to accept the honour was in his eyes an act of rebellion against the Emperor. Although the Court of Directors concurred in the policy of the Supreme Government, it is easy to see

[1] Summary, &c., p. 12.

that the Anglo-Indian opinion was opposed to it, as a step which outraged Muhammadan sentiment without affording any compensating advantages [1].

The Governor-General's policy with regard to the Mughal Emperor is interesting, and is explained at some length in his Private Journal. In the early part of 1815 he was close to Delhi, and it was intimated to him that he ought to proceed there to visit that sovereign. But he refused, because 'His Majesty expected my acquiescence in a ceremonial which was to imply an acknowledgment that he was the liege-lord of the British possessions.' He denied that the Company held territory on this dependent tenure, not only because he considered it was impolitic to keep up the fiction that the Emperor was lord-paramount of India, but because 'of the recent Act of Parliament which declares the sovereignty of the Company's possession to be in the British Crown.'

> 'The house of Timúr,' he goes on to say, 'had been put so much out of sight, that all habit of adverting to it was failing fast in India; and nothing has kept the floating notion of a duty owed to the imperial family but our gratuitous and persevering exhibition of their pretensions—an exhibition attended with much servile obeisance in the etiquette imposed upon us by the ceremonial of the court. I have thence held it right to discountenance any pretension of the sort, either as it applies to us or to any of the native princes.'

The act of homage is in India performed by a

[1] Malcolm's *History of India*, i. 537; Summary, &c., p. 43.

present, called *Nazzur*, which the inferior offers in public to the superior; it had been the habit for the Resident at Delhi to present the Mughal Emperor, on certain occasions, with a Nazzur, in the name of the Governor-General. But Lord Hastings refused to allow this custom to continue, and did away with it, 'considering such a public testimony of dependence and subservience as irreconcileable to any rational policy[1].'

It should, however, be stated that the Government of Calcutta coined money which bore the effigy of the Delhi Emperor, and that Lord Hastings appears to have made no attempt to abolish this proceeding, which survived until the time when the Crown formally assumed the direct government of India, without the interposition of the East India Company. It would seem therefore that the Governor-General had no leisure to go thoroughly into the question, and contented himself by ignoring the fictitious supremacy of the Mughal Emperor, and by encouraging his principal vassals to throw off a technical allegiance which might be eventually dangerous to British power.

It has already been remarked that one of the defects of the subsidiary and protective system, introduced by Wellesley and completed by Lord Hastings, was the difficulty of dealing with native princes who persistently refused to discharge the duties of government. Impossible as it was to abstain from interference where misrule assumed proportions which amounted to a

[1] Private Journal, i. 318 and 323.

public calamity, it was also very puzzling to know how to apply an efficient remedy; for, contrary as it may appear to the pre-conceptions of some, it is nevertheless a fact that successive governments in India have been extremely reluctant to absorb territory, and have invariably delayed this sometimes necessary proceeding as long as it was possible to do so. Unless, then, the offending prince was deposed and another placed on the throne,—obviously a step which could only be taken in the most extreme and exceptional cases,—either British officers had temporarily to assume the administration of the country, or a native minister had to be found who could take the reins of government into his hands with some prospect of success. The former of these alternatives was objectionable; it was a violent remedy, and made it difficult to revert to native rule. The latter was also highly undesirable, for it placed the country in irresponsible hands, and gave the minister who was selected for this delicate task—and who had naturally to be supported while he undertook it—a power and position which was too often abused. An instance occurred in the state of Haidarábád, which, producing painful and undeserved consequences to Lord Hastings, illustrates the complex problems which surrounded a Governor-General of India at that time, and the difficulties of his position.

The Nizám had unfortunately proved himself to be utterly incapable of ruling, owing to which disorganisation had prevailed in the principality to such an extent, that it was found necessary to confide the administration to the only native who seemed fitted to undertake it, a man named Chandu Lal. It soon became apparent that the new minister, though capable and industrious, was rapacious and extravagant, and, as a consequence, the finances of the state fell into the utmost confusion, the inhabitants were plundered and overburdened with exactions, and society became demoralised and was on the verge of dissolution. Sir Charles Metcalfe, who had been appointed Resident, November 1820, when this disorder was at its height, endeavoured to control the minister, but with little success, and the financial distress augmenting, it became a question whether the state would not be involved in bankruptcy.

Meanwhile Chandu Lal had contracted heavy debts with an English firm which had been established at Haidarábád under the name of Palmer and Co. It was represented that this house was ready to advance loans at a more reasonable rate of interest than the native bankers were willing to do, and on this supposition, considerable sums had been lent to the Nizám to relieve him of the embarrassments of his position. By an Act of Parliament, passed in 1796 for the purpose of checking abuses which had been occasioned by Europeans in their pecuniary dealings in India, it was declared illegal for British subjects to offer loans to native princes, except with the express permission of the Governor-General; in 1816, Lord Hastings, having been led to believe that the transactions of the firm with the court of Haidarábád were beneficial to the latter and to the Company, granted the necessary consent; but he also stipulated that the Supreme Government could not undertake any pledge for the security of the sums advanced, or become entangled in discussions with the Nizám for the recovery of the debt.

In May, 1820, Chandu Lal proposed for the Resident's sanction, the negotiation with Palmer and Co. of a much larger loan than usual, amounting to sixty lakhs of rupees, and asserted that the money was required for objects that clearly seemed to benefit the Nizám. The necessary authority was granted, but on the facts becoming known to the Court of Directors, they, remembering past abuses, disapproved of all the transactions with the firm in question, and directed that the Governor-General's consent should be withdrawn. These instructions were obeyed; but the suspicions of Sir Charles Metcalfe, (who by this time had reached Haidarábád), being aroused, he proceeded to examine into the affairs of the principality, and he was startled to find that the large sums obtained from Palmer and Co., which reached to nearly a million sterling, were wasted, and had been improperly applied, and that the exactions made upon the wretched inhabitants were still continued with unrelenting rigour. Thereupon a strict inquiry was instituted, and it was then ascertained that the dealings of this financial house formed no exception to those which the Act (already mentioned) had been framed to prohibit, that the rate of interest was exorbitant, and as much as 24 per cent., and that the sixty lakhs had not been applied to the purposes for which they had been ostensibly borrowed. When these facts were realised, the Indian Government withdrew its countenance from the firm, the minister was directed to close his account there, and a tribute payable to the Nizám by the Company for the possession of the Northern Circars was capitalised into the necessary million, to liberate the court of Haidarábád from all further business with the house of Palmer and Co.

Until the scandal was revealed, Lord Hastings had all this time been firmly convinced that these financial transactions constituted the best and indeed the only feasible expedient for extricating the Nizám's principality from its embarrassments, and for re-establishing it in a state of solvency; in consenting to countenance a European house of business, he relied altogether upon the judgment of the former Resident, who strongly recommended the adoption of the course pursued, and whose official position, long experience, and intimate knowledge of the Nizám's affairs might be trusted to form a sound and impartial opinion on the subject. Such was the Governor-General's confidence in the discretion of the Political Agent and in his own decisions, that he was slow to believe that this opinion was faulty, or that he himself could be mistaken; and when Sir Charles Metcalfe represented the true state of the case, he came at first to the hasty and erroneous conclusion that the investigation was imperfectly conducted and based upon prejudice. As soon however as he suspected the truth, he hastened to condemn what he had formerly approved, and expressed his strong sense of the impropriety which had been committed. But his reluctance to acknowledge an error had been misunderstood, and when he avowed a remote interest in the prosperity of the firm (by imprudently declaring that one of the partners, husband of his ward to whom he was much attached, was a friend he would be glad to serve), a forced and unjust construction was put on the avowal which was wholly unauthorised by the facts.

Nor is it improbable that many of the members of the Court of Directors were not indisposed to seize the opportunity to attack a Governor-General whose policy they deeply resented, but whose success they were forced to applaud. And thus it came about that an unjustifiable conclusion was hastily formed, to the effect that he had been influenced by personal motives in countenancing the financial operations of Palmer and Co. No accusation to this effect was made, but the very indirectness of the charge made it the more difficult to refute, and weighed heavily upon a man who, whatever his faults might have been, had nothing sordid in his character, and who was ever conspicuous for uprightness, and for the scrupulous honesty of all his acts. It is easy to conceive how such a suspicion must have wounded deeply the sensitive and proud nature of a person of Lord

Hastings' temperament, who, conscious of no fault, found himself thus assailed in a way that touched him to the quick.

An angry correspondence ensued, and in 1825, after a stormy debate in the Court of Proprietors, the communications from the Board of Directors to the Bengal Government on this subject were approved by a large majority. The proceedings were painful, and displayed a latent spirit of ungenerous antipathy to one whose career was spotless and who was smarting under the mortification of having been himself deceived. But they were useful, for they entirely vindicated Lord Hastings' integrity, in a manner which—in view of the imputation suggested—was necessary, and which nothing else could have done so amply and conclusively.

The Directors, while making captious and irrelevant criticisms, adopted too often, in this unfortunate episode, a tone of suspicion and resentment towards an exalted official and conspicuously successful statesman, for which it is difficult to account. But on the other hand, it is indisputable that, with greater experience than the Governor-General of the corrupting influences which India too often exercised over some Europeans in the early days of British occupation there, they exercised a wise discretion in putting an end to the financial transactions, even before they found out the impropriety which had been practised; and by the zeal they displayed to purge their public administration of abuses, they discharged a duty of no small importance to the Company's welfare and of the greatest consequence to the natives subjected to British rule [1].

[1] Wilson, viii. 486, &c., from which this account has been mainly taken; Auber, ii. 559; Marshman, ii. 368. Prinsep attributes some of the difficulties that occurred in Haidarábád to the fact that an irresponsible minister, even with the assistance of an able British Resident, is unable to supervise the affairs of so large a principality as that belonging to the Nizám. Prinsep, ii. 414.

CHAPTER X

ADMINISTRATIVE REFORMS; CONCLUSION; LORD HASTINGS' WORK IN INDIA

BESIDES the many changes, reconstituting fundamentally British rule in India, which marked the period 1813–23, reforms were also introduced in the domestic administration of the country that cannot be altogether passed over. The East India Company had been from time to time subjected to certain alterations in the Royal Charter which controlled its rights and defined its duties in the territories that were assigned to its management. In 1813 a new Charter was granted to which allusion has been incidentally made in the Fourth Chapter of this volume[1]; before granting it, however, a searching inquiry had been held into the whole of the Company's administration; and as the conclusion arrived at was that the Judicial and Revenue systems were capable of improvement, it was proposed to reform them as soon as possible. Lord Hastings was not the man to delay useful work of this nature, and his natural desire to remove grievances as well as his indomitable energy both urged him to correct abuses

[1] See *ante*, p. 83.

and to introduce measures which were calculated to bring about the prosperity and the happiness of the people committed to his charge.

It should be premised that domestic policy, including judicial and fiscal administration, differed in the three Presidencies, and that these matters were independently controlled by the governments which had been established there. It should further be observed that British rule having prevailed in the provinces of Bengal for a longer time than had been the case elsewhere, a certain policy had been already adopted, which rendered any sweeping reform more difficult of execution than in the territories which had only lately come under the Company's government. Hence when changes were found to be necessary they could only be gradually introduced, and extreme caution had to be taken to ensure the people against the evils that invariably follow a hasty or ill-considered amendment in the established laws and customs. In Madras and Bombay, government had a freer hand, and the experience already gained in Bengal enabled the authorities in these two Presidencies to respond with greater promptitude to the necessities of the position, as well as to the suggestions which were made in England.

The first point we shall mention is the business in the courts of Civil Judicature, where by reason of the paucity of the judges, of the increasing number and prosperity of the inhabitants, and of the popularity of the tribunals under British control, work was much in arrears[1]. It was not easy to augment the number of English judges, for the cost of maintaining Europeans who were not indigenous to the country was prohibitory to any such arrangement. Natives had certainly been invested with judicial powers ever since 1793, but as they were badly paid and kept in an unduly subordinate position, they lost their self-respect and became too often inefficient and corrupt. To correct this state of things, the Board of Control proposed that the old native institutions should be revived by restoring the functions of the village head-men and local arbitrators, called *Panchayats.*

The Government of Bengal found the proposal impracticable, for these institutions had been partially destroyed by the revenue settlements that had been made in the Presidency; a remedy therefore was sought in another direction, viz. by improving the pay and position of the native judges, by enlarging their powers, by subjecting them to more efficient supervision, and by adding to their number. The instructions from home were however carried out in Madras, where the village organization was in better state of preservation; but the result was curious, for the people preferred the native and English tribunals and deserted those provided for them in their own communities. In Bombay, however, where no other

[1] In 1810 there were 135,553 cases pending, but in 1815 the number decreased to 108,286, making nevertheless a formidable list of arrears; Wilson, viii. 509. See, moreover, p. 508, &c. of this volume, from which the greater part of this chapter has been taken.

form of arbitration was known, the courts of the head-men and *Panchayats* were not similarly deserted, and the proposals emanating from England were not unsuccessful.

The Board of Control also came to the conclusion that it would be expedient to undo the administration established by Lord Cornwallis (who separated the functions of the Collectors from those of the criminal Judges), and to re-unite in one person fiscal and police duties; in order to carry out this reform, it was moreover necessary to vest the zamíndárs with authority, and to give additional powers to the native revenue officers. The Government of Bengal in this instance also found the proposed change unadvisable, as calculated to oppress the people; for it was not believed that the rapacity of the native element could be restrained from exacting more than was due [1]. The following remarks from Lord Hastings' Private Journal touches upon this subject, and may be reproduced, to show how disastrous it would have been to increase the powers of the zamíndárs over the people :—

'It was assumed that the zamíndárs were the real landowners, and that, commanding as such the attachment of the peasantry, they would insure the adherence of the latter to our government if their interest in the land were secured from precariousness or extortion. On this principle the proprietary rights of the zamíndár to the tract under his management was declared, subject to his paying in perpetuity to govern-

[1] Examples of organised rapacity of the native officers are given in the Private Journal, ii. 106; see also Marshman, ii. 361.

ment a quit-rent settled generally by the rate at which he was actually assessed . . . It was forgotten that he was not the cultivator, and no protection was given to the ráyat, the real tiller (perhaps the real proprietor) of the soil, against the oppressive exactions of the zamíndár, whose actual dependent he was made by this settlement. In fact, the zamíndár was originally nothing more than the contractor with the native government for the rent of a certain district. . . . Where the rent demanded from him was high, he looked to discharge it as well as provide for his own maintenance by squeezing the ráyat[1].'

The changes introduced into the criminal system in Bengal were therefore confined to an enlargement of the powers (with increased supervision) of the native magistrates, enabling them to deal with cases which had hitherto been decided by the Circuit Judges, and to the introduction of an improved set of police regulations, with the object of securing greater activity and of guarding against abuses of power which had too often taken place. In Madras and Bombay, however, the condition of the people was different, and the new criminal system recommended from home was established in those Presidencies.

In alluding to the principles which guided fiscal policy, it should be remembered that Asiatic revenue differs from European taxation, where certain imposts, and no more, are laid upon the people for the sole purpose of defraying the public services of the nation. In India, on the contrary, the revenue is a fixed and

[1] Private Journal, ii. 62.

constant quantity, and is the property of the ruler, who utilizes it, or as much of it as he thinks necessary, to maintain the administration of the state. In the former case, Government is the trustee of the people, liable to be called to account and to find its supplies cut off; whereas in the latter, the sovereign is their master or irresponsible protector, liable indeed to be checked by violence, but whose taxes cannot be legally withheld. In the East, the revenue is derived mainly from a contribution levied off the land, the remainder being raised by monopolies, and partially by indirect taxation such as prevails in Europe. The contributions from the land and monopolies may of course vary, but the principle is unchangeable, and in so far the revenue cannot alter [1].

In the lower Bengal provinces, the land revenue had already been assessed (1793) by a permanent settlement, and here little change took place during the period, 1813–23, now under review. But where no permanent settlement had existed, the Governor-General found that, owing to the absence of proper surveys, great injustice would have been done had it been introduced too hastily. Opposed as he was to the zamíndári system, he found it impossible to contract directly with the numerous cultivators in districts where a teeming population existed, and accordingly engagements were made with the representatives of each village community for the whole of the government's claim. The community itself assessed

[1] Prinsep, ii. 422.

the peasants for their proper share, subject to an appeal in the courts, if there was a dispute. The practice thus adopted appeared to be satisfactory, and it was rendered the more so by the vigorous efforts made to correct all abuses which manifested themselves. Meanwhile active steps were also taken to ascertain accurately the state and value of the land, the boundaries and nature of private rights, and the tenures of the various persons who were interested. It is evident that this information—necessary for the conclusion of an equitable settlement—could not be gained immediately, and though only acquired and digested long after the period in which we are now concerned, the fact that this great and important woık was promoted in Lord Hastings' time deserves mention in this volume.

In the Madras Presidency, Sir Thomas Munro, who became Governor in 1820, introduced and carried the ráyatwári system—by which the cultivators of the soil became the direct payers of revenue, without the intervention of either a zamíndár or the village community—and this form of tenure prevails to the present day[1]; at the same time the peasants were relieved of unjust exactions to which in the past they had been obliged to submit. In Bombay, Government was principally occupied in making investigations, and the settlement begun was founded on the village system, where the head-men made the

[1] See Hunter's *Indian Empire, &c.*, Ed. 1882, p. 340.

assessment, subject to certain restraints to prevent oppression.

The general financial results achieved by Lord Hastings were highly satisfactory, and despite the difficulties which surrounded Government in 1813, show a marked and decided improvement on that year, both in increased receipts and in efficiency of administration. The charges upon Government had also naturally increased, but in a less proportion to the additional revenue acquired, so that after providing for the public debt, a clear surplus of more than three millions sterling had been obtained, and this notwithstanding the fact that two wars of the first magnitude had been undertaken, the cost of which weighed heavily upon the resources of the country. The following short table will show this account:—

	1813–14.	1822–23.
Receipts	£17,228,000	23,120,000
Expenditure (charges, interest on public debt, &c.) . . .	15,270,000	19,776,000
Surplus	£1,958,000	3,344,000[1]

Increase receipts in 1822–23 over 1813–14, £5,892,000.

The increasing prosperity showed itself in many ways. The Government bonds which in 1813 were twelve per cent. discount, stood at a premium of

[1] Wilson, viii. Appendix vii. The military charges 1809–10 to 1813–14 averaged £7,344,000; in the next two years (Nepál War) £8,840,000; in the next five years (Maráthá War) £9,770,000; and in 1822–23 £8,405,000. *Ibid.* viii. 561.

fourteen per cent. in 1823. More supplies were sent to England; for while during the twenty years preceding 1813, an average of not quite half a million had been sent home, during the eight years beginning with 1814 the average was a little over a million sterling, and during the five years 1814–18, inclusive, it had been a much larger amount. The public debt had certainly increased by about five millions and a half; but the cash balances in the various treasuries in 1821 exceeded the sum in hand in 1814, by six millions and a quarter. The additional debt, raised during Lord Hastings' administration, might have been easily paid off, but the Governor-General 'deemed it highly impolitic to break a tie which so obviously secures the attachment of the monied class to our government, in a country where that class has peculiar influence.' He observed, moreover, that the native princes were investing their money in Indian securities, 'a motive the more for them to abstain from intrigues against us.' These advantages were gained without the imposition of any new tax, 'while several teasing demands were abolished, as well in the old provinces as in the acquired territories,' and without curtailing the expenditure devoted to public works for the development of the country[1].

'The government of India,' says Mr. Wilson, 'overcame all its financial difficulties, and upon the restoration of peace was provided with ample means to meet every demand. At no

[1] Summary, &c., p. 29, &c.; Marshman, ii. 364.

previous period in the history of the country was the credit of the British Government more firmly established, or was the prospect of financial prosperity more promising than at the commencement of 1823, when the Marquess of Hastings retired from the guidance of the pecuniary interests of India[1].'

Very few chaplains, amounting to only thirty-two in the whole of India, were provided for the spiritual needs of the numerous English population that was constrained to live in Asia in the Company's service; this matter had not escaped notice, and Lord Hastings frequently observes in his Private Journal with regret and surprise, that there was an almost entire absence of places of worship in the country. The renewal of the Charter in 1813 gave an opportunity for applying a remedy to this state of things, and the matter was not neglected; though the measures taken effected little with respect to conversions, yet they gave an impetus to general education among the natives. The Governor-General cordially approved of this latter work, promoted it in every way in his power, and established schools out of his own private means. He was the first to encourage the moral and intellectual improvement of the natives, and his views on the subject were altogether in advance of Indian officials of his time.

Soon after the Nepál war he took an early opportunity of proclaiming his anxiety to raise the people

[1] Wilson, viii. 564.

committed to his care by education, and his repudiation of the narrow policy which unfortunately animated so many Europeans who lived in India.

'This Government,' he said, 'will never be influenced by the erroneous position that to spread information among men is to render them less tractable and less submissive to authority. . . . It would be treason against British sentiment to imagine that it ever could be the principle of this Government to perpetuate ignorance in order to secure paltry and dishonest advantages over the blindness of the multitude [1].'

Again, commenting upon some brutal and deliberate crimes commited by sepoys he says:—

'The gain of four or five rupees or the gratification of the most petty pique, seems quite enough to urge the sepoy to the cold-blooded murder of his fellow-soldier and intimate companion. The cause lies in this, that the perpetrator has no conception of the atrocity of the act. Let this be the answer to those who contend that it is unwise to disseminate instruction among the multitude. Absence of instruction necessarily implies destitution of morality. God be praised, we have been successful in extinguishing a system of rapine which was not only the unremitting scourge of an immense population, but depraved its habits by example, and inflicted necessities, while it stood an obstacle to every kind of improvement. It is befitting the British name and character that advantage should be taken of the opening which we have effected, and that establishments should be introduced or stimulated by us which may rear a rising generation in some knowledge of social duties [2].'

[1] Marshman, ii. 357.
[2] Private Journal, ii. 325.

These views joined to the general liberality of his character led him to remove the restrictions which had before his time fettered the freedom of the Indian press; he moreover allowed newspapers to circulate at a reduced rate of postage, and it was during his administration that the first native journal appeared in print.

Keenly interesting himself in all with whom he came into contact, he endeavoured to raise the officers of the Company's armies to a higher status than they enjoyed, more befitting their position. Wielding great power, incurring grave responsibilities, engaged in subjecting a vast continent to the rule of their country, their services were often unrequited and their military rank, in many cases, córresponded inadequately with the onerous functions they were called upon to discharge. Just before the Maráthá war, some of the commanders of divisions, who up to that time had never been given a higher rank than that of colonel, were promoted brigadier-generals; and when the extension of the Order of the Bath was instituted, fifteen officers of the Indian forces were raised to the dignity of Knight Commander, on account of the 'eminent services which have been rendered to the empire' by that army. Sir D. Ochterlony was subsequently invested (March, 1818) by Lord Hastings with the ribbon of the Grand Cross, who pronounced upon that occasion the following words:—

'You have obliterated a distinction painful for the officers of the Honourable Company, and you have opened the door for your brothers in arms to a reward which their recent display of exalted spirit and invincible intrepidity proves could not be more deservedly extended to the officers of any army on earth[1].'

Nor was it only the Europeans to whom he sought to render justice. Rising above the prejudices of the day, he admitted to Government House those half-castes, whose position entitled them to consideration, and endeavoured to gain their good-will by proving to them that, at all events in his eyes, colour was no bar to his favour. Half-castes were in a peculiar position; and many of them, though in strong sympathy with British ideas, were despised and ungenerously treated by the European community; and yet as they had entire knowledge of native prejudices and were in intimate relations with popular sentiments, they formed no unimportant link between the governing classes and the governed. Lord Hastings adopted a course that might be expected from a man of his enlightened character, and rewarded those who were in the public service, and who deserved it, by promoting them to a position which would enable them to give their best services to the British Government. He tells the story with regard to a celebrated leader of Irregular horse, a half-caste, in the following manner:—

'I then desired to see Captain Skinner. Private information had been given me that he had become dissatisfied with

[1] Thornton's *British Empire in India*, p. 456.

our service and proposed to resign. He is a half-caste, and was formerly in the Maráthá service. On the war breaking out with them (the second Maráthá war), he quitted their service in consequence of the proclamation recalling all British subjects, was employed by us, and much distinguished himself by his enterprise, his intrepidity, and his judgment. At the peace the corps commanded by him was kept in pay, and he was retained at its head, at the frontier station of Hánsi. The equity and the strict observance of every promise which had marked Captain Skinner for many years, had obtained for him a prodigious influence among the natives. The loss of such a man would be serious, especially as there was little probability that he could reconcile his mind to idleness, and it is sure that he would have most tempting offers from Holkar or Sindhia. His discontent arose from this, that the officers of Irregulars have no rank but in their own corps. Hence, if the garrison of native infantry at Hánsi be reduced (as has often been the case) to a subaltern's party, Captain Skinner must find himself under the orders of possibly a very inexperienced youth. I affected not to know anything of the dispositions which he had indulged; but, beginning by a compliment to the state of his corps, I told him I wished to give a public mark of my estimation of his character. I therefore requested he would assume the honorary title of Lieutenant-Colonel; and I apprized him of my intention to propose to Government that such a rank in the Irregulars should entitle the officer holding it to rank as youngest field-officer of the line, and to command all captains and subalterns. I explained that as battalions were often commanded by captains, it would be easy to compose such a corps for an irregular officer in whom one had confidence, as might enable him to achieve actions meriting the highest distinctions and recompense. He appeared extraordinarily gratified, and with peculiar earnestness entreated me to rely on his unreserved devotion. To understand this warmth of feeling, one ought to know the excessive depression in which half-castes are held by the Company's servants[1].'

A brief note should not be omitted in this volume, to record the public works which were undertaken during the administration under review. Roads, bridges, and canals were constructed or repaired, and the communications throughout the country were improved, by which the internal commerce was promoted and agricultural industry encouraged. Delhi, in the last century, had been supplied with good water by a canal which the Mughals had made; but the works had fallen into decay for many a long year, and as the Jumna, on which the city is situated, passes over great beds of natron, the inhabitants were condemned to use the brackish water which was all they could get. Lord Hastings caused this canal to be opened up, and thus Delhi was indebted to him for a gratuitous and plentiful supply of pure water drawn from the spot where the Jumna issues from the mountains, before it enters into the plains. He also restored two other canals, one, which ran into the province of Hariána, and another which traversed the Doáb. The districts moreover through which these water-courses went, were once again rendered fit for human habitation.

Calcutta, the seat of government, was in a very unhealthy state, and though Lord Wellesley had done

[1] Private Journal, i. 293.

a good deal to improve the town when he was Governor-General, his works and plans were suspended after he left India. Lord Hastings, however, turned his attention to this subject, and having made an investigation into the causes of its unsanitary condition, he devoted large sums of money in beautifying the town, in rendering it more healthy and more adapted to the requirements of Eastern life, and in erecting a handsome embankment along the river. He further planned the construction of a secure water-way between the mouth of the Húglí and Calcutta, where there were dangerous shoals, which impeded the navigation and obstructed the free circulation of trade to the Indian capital[1].

There was scarcely a matter of any importance connected with India in which Lord Hastings did not exhibit a profound interest, and his extraordinary energy forced him to attempt to regulate every question that presented itself before him. In spite of his age, no man ever worked harder than he, or devoted himself more unremittingly to his duties, and he continued his labours without intermission, during the nine years he remained at the head of the government which was intrusted to his care.

In short, his administration marks an epoch in the internal development of the country, when the finances were put in order, when India was brought more closely within the fold of the national family, and when the foundations of domestic reform were laid.

[1] Marshman, ii. 375; Summary, &c., 36.

From this time forward, the native has been taken by the hand, his moral well-being has been regarded as a duty, and gradually has he been brought into contact with European ideas of social duties, and prepared for the reception of a higher form of civilization.

All this progress cannot be justly ascribed to the personal initiative of the Governor-General; but the measures that produced it had his cordial assent, and were advocated and promoted by his expansive sympathy and zealous industry. His title to the gratitude of the nation does not however rest upon these achievements, great though they were; but is founded on a higher claim, namely, on what he did for the consolidation of the Indian Empire.

When he reached Calcutta, English possessions were disjointed and fragmentary, long frontiers had to be guarded and maintained, communications between the parts were uncertain and difficult, rapid access to many of the provinces impossible. These territories were in contact with turbulent and hostile neighbours, and were exposed to the desolating effects of unchecked violence, and to the ruin and misery caused by inroads of predatory hordes. The Maráthá communities were in a state of anarchy, their rule was one of devastation, it was continually destroying and never repairing [1]. The numerous bands of free-booters and mercenary troops that infested the country crushed the inhabitants and sorely embarrassed govern-

[1] Opinion of Sir T. Munro; Auber, ii. 529.

ment within the Company's borders. Development was checked, peace was precarious, and the stability of British authority was in imminent peril of being overturned and annihilated.

All this was changed by the Marquess of Hastings. The hostility of Nepál was overcome, and the northern frontier was secured. The Maráthá combination against British rule and the predatory system which threatened the Company's territories were annihilated. Central India was settled and pacified. In a word, the independent native states who conceived in 1813 that they could expel the English from India were defeated, and in 1823 every prince in that vast region up to the Sutlej was brought into subjection to the Government of Calcutta [1].

Wellesley had had a similar problem to face, and he originated a vigorous policy to solve it; he put his plans into execution, but he was not allowed to conclude them. Lord Hastings was theoretically opposed to this policy; yet he had hardly set foot in India, before he realised its importance and its absolute necessity, if the British nation were to continue its mission in the East.

'It was by preponderance of power,' he wrote to England in 1815, 'that those mines of wealth had been acquired for the Company's treasure, and by preponderance of power alone could they be retained. The supposition that the British power could discard the means of strength and yet enjoy the fruits of it, was one that would certainly be speedily

[1] Summary, &c., p. 35.

dissipated; in the state of India, were we to be feeble our rule would be a dream, and a very short one[1].'

The scheme for producing the pacification of India was not his conception; but having approved of its merit, he adopted it as his own, and, more fortunate than his great predecessor, he was able to take large and comprehensive measures to bring it to a successful conclusion. Essentially a man of action, his resolute will bore down all opposition to his well-matured plans. The breadth of his policy, the vigour of his intellect, the sagacity of his measures, and the skill of his operations, surprised his enemies, overcame their resistance, reconciled them to his authority, and effected his purpose in every detail.

The Indian Continent was reduced to order, the irregularities in the Company's territories were gradually removed, its possessions were consolidated, and the paramount position of England was assured. The settlement which the Marquess of Hastings made has been modified, but it has never been undone; his work was thorough, far-reaching and comprehensive. Modern India is largely based upon the results which he attained. The period of his administration forms an era in the history of our advance in the East, which marks the end of a halting policy and the dawn of a new order, when Great Britain finally assumed undivided responsibility for, and supreme control over, the Empire of Continental India.

[1] Auber, ii. 552.

INDEX

THE END.